Frederick Forsyth

A Matter of Protocol

Frederick Forsyth
A Matter of Protocol

Craig Cabell

Foreword by Lord Janner of Braunstone, QC

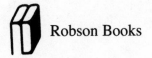 Robson Books

First published in Great Britain in 2001 by
Robson Books, 10 Blenheim Court,
Brewery Road, London N7 9NY

A member of the Chrysalis Group plc

British Library Cataloguing in Publication Data
A catalogue record for this title is available from the British Library.

ISBN 1 86105 414 9

Typeset in Times by FiSH Books, London WC1.
Printed and bound in Great Britain by Butler & Tanner Ltd, Frome and London

Contents

Author's Note   vii

Acknowledgements   ix

Foreword by Greville Janner –
    Lord Janner of Brunstone, QC   xiii

Introduction A Lesson in Faction   1

Part One The Forsyth Story   7

1   The Adventurer   9

2   Heads Around Doors   18

3   Hush-a-Biafra   31

4   Winter of Discontent?   35

Part Two The Forsyth Novels   37

5   The Mysterious Jackal   39

6   Hunting Nazi War Criminals   47

7   Unleashing *The Dogs of War*   57

8   A Christmas Ghost Story   64

9   When the Devil Drives   68

10   *No Comebacks*   74

11   A Nuclear Suitcase   78

12   *The Negotiator*   84

13 '...a sort of unleashed Ghenkhis Khan'   89
14 Qubeth-ut-Allah   97
15 *Icon*   104
16 Not the Usual Fare   109
17 Dinner in the West End   115
18 *The Veteran*   120
19 Enter *Draco*   132
20 The World of Frederick Forsyth   135

Part Three The Forsyth Legacy   139
Mixing Business and Pleasure: An Interview with Ed Victor 143
Frederick Forsyth: Thoughts and Opinions   146
Frederick Forsyth Film Guide   152
Frederick Forsyth Bibliography   193

Appendices   199

Author's Note

IT WAS in March 2000 that I decided to write a Frederick Forsyth biography. I called Freddie up to request an interview to support a freelance article I was writing and we duly met the following day.

After the interview, I put the biography idea to him and he told me that he had turned down approximately 150 similar proposals from biographers over the years, mainly because they wanted to get 'too close'.

However, what I proposed was a 'man and his works' biography, which looked closely at his life up to the release of *The Day of the Jackal* (fascinating in itself) and then studied his books in more detail from there.

'A slim volume, more of an extended CV,' he mused. He then agreed, asking to approve the biography section when completed. This he duly did but he also helped with various other aspects of the book. For example, when I was having problems tracking down Edward Fox for interview, I called Freddie and he said, 'Leave it with me.' The following day I received a phone call from Edward Fox and we duly met up.

With Frederick Forsyth apparently winding down his career as a novelist, it seemed an opportune time to celebrate his success as a writer, neatly tying the biography in with the 30th anniversary of the release of *The Day of the Jackal*. The resulting book stands as a celebration of one of Britain's most successful – but modest – thriller writers.

Craig Cabell
London, June 2001

Acknowledgements

Many people, in both large and small ways, have assisted me in the writing of this book. I would like to acknowledge and thank all those I have quoted from: Lord Janner of Braunstone, QC, Lord Andrew Lloyd-Webber, Michael Heseltine, Sir Derek Jacobi, Edward Fox, Ed Victor, John 'Cats Eyes' Cunningham, Dennis 'Hurricane' David, George Jesse Turner, Campbell Armstrong, Craig Thomas, Ian Rankin and the great Roald Dahl.

Special thanks go to the usual crew: my wife Anita, my parents Shirley and Colin, my in-laws Berny and Dave; for their support in many different ways. Thanks also to Mavis and Ian Dow for their constant encouragement.

I would also like to acknowledge 'The Magnificent Seven' for their companionship and opinions: James Lau, Richard Ball, Eamon Exley, Mark Ottowell, Steve Hope, Graham Thomas and Martin Procter. Thanks also to John Jeffery, for hearty conversation over the odd glass of wine and Mr James Davy for supplying it. Also special thanks are due to Alan Hunter for his thoughts, opinions and for downloading *Quintet*.

I would also like to express my gratitude to both Doreen Porter and Tracey Allen for their professionalism and enthusiasm, always above and beyond the call of duty.

Thanks are also due to Lorna Russell, the British Film Institute, Flashbacks Movie Store, Chivers Press, Baggin's Book Bazaar, Twiggers booksearch, Brian Aldrich, Dorothy Henning at *Reader's Digest*, Catherine Trippett and Denise Bontoft at Random House Archive and Library, Carmel Fitzgerald at Transworld for supplying some of the research material in part three of this book, and Rachel Grindrod at Transworld for clarifying copyright issues.

Finally, my heartfelt thanks go to Frederick Forsyth himself, for not only allowing me to write this authorised biography about his life and work but for also being so generous in his support, from interview time (and the loan of photographs) through to approval of the biography section.

Craig Cabell
July 2000

For Anita, Samantha and Nathan
With much love

'When I was a cub reporter on an English provincial newspaper, I came under the tutelage of a wonderful teacher, the chief reporter of the office. He impressed on me two maxims, "Get the facts right", and "Tell it the way it was".'

Prologue (written in Ireland, February 1976) to
The Making of an African Legend: The Biafra Story,
Frederick Forsyth

Foreword

IN REAL life, Frederick Forsyth is as entertaining, provocative and as focused as his novels. It is good that Craig Cabell has at last lifted some of the mystery surrounding that life.

Too many celebrities are great fun on stage or on paper, but sadly uninspiring as companions. Not Freddie Forsyth. I wish that the Left had as vocal and articulate an advocate as the Right enjoys in Freddie. But as we are both democrats, we can agree that in a joyfully free country such as ours, one of its greatest writers is entitled on occasion to be wrong.

It was Nazi gold not politics that brought the two of us together. I had read his brilliantly researched epic, *The Odessa File*. And when in 1996, documents found by the World Jewish Congress in the US archives revealed – after 50 years in darkness – some of the disgraceful involvement of Swiss banks in the use of Nazi gold, I read the book. Here, written decades before, was the hideous story of the escape of the SS murderers through 'the rat run', financed by Nazi gold.

In Craig Cabell's book, he recounts how Forsyth regrets not having spent more space on this evil tale. No matter. That small source helped to irrigate a remarkable, international investigation and campaign, which has led to at least some of the survivors of the SS and their collaborators achieving at least some measure of justice and restitution.

So it is an honour to be a friend of Frederick Forsyth – and to salute him. And we must be grateful to Craig Cabell for throwing public light on to the extraordinary life of this rightly acclaimed and most excellent novelist. Oh yes, most importantly, *The Odessa File* should be required reading for every student. It stands alongside *Schindler's List* as a tower of tragedy – truth in the form of fiction – evil incarnate, written with unconcealed and passionate reality.

Greville Janner
Lord Janner of Brunstone, QC

Introduction
A Lesson in Faction

'Like most rich and successful men, he had three lives: his
public and professional life... his private life, which is not
necessarily what it means... and his secret life.'

No Comebacks
Frederick Forsyth

KIMBERLEY PLACED the zip drive tape into his jacket pocket.
He pulled up the collar of his seen-better-days Pinstripe and
stepped out into the London rain.

Quickly, he crossed Blackfriars Bridge and followed the north-
bank footpath that snaked its way, parallel to the Thames, down
towards Westminster.

He didn't quite reach Westminster, choosing to cross the road
shortly after Hungerford Bridge and cut down Horse Guards
Avenue towards the Ministry of Defence.

He didn't walk inside, even though it was his place of work.
Instead, he crossed the road and walked into the Old War Office
building, flashing his pass to a vigil guard as he did so.

Once he had negotiated the security booth with his own
exclusive pass number, Kimberley dropped the collar of his

jacket and brushed himself down. The rain had been light, only leaving a damp film on his suit.

He then walked confidently through a maze of antique-looking corridors, eventually passing building security and a chunk of the Berlin Wall – Christ knows what that was doing there – however, Old War Office corridors were scattered with a vast assortment of relics of historical value; and that was just the staff.

Kimberley walked through a set of swing doors and immediately entered an office to his right.

A fat middle-aged man wearing a wide-collared shirt, prised himself out of a battered swivel chair.

Kimberley closed the door as Fatso Douglas moved round the desk to shake hands.

'Always a pleasure, Hugh,' Fatso said in his usual nasal voice.

'Not this time, Gerry,' Kimberley said, refusing the hand. 'Mr Moonlight has just presented me with the zip 100 copy of the photographs.'

'Photographs?' Gerry replied. 'What photographs?'

'Oh, come on, Gerry,' Kimberley said, taking a seat at his former colleague's desk. 'The ones of you screwing Lord Sandford's wife, of course.'

Kimberley now sat with his back to Gerry Douglas. He was playing with a silver-plated model of a B2 Stealth bomber; a presentation from an American Air Force Consortium after the first British B2 airshow flight in 1999.

Gerry moved – more slowly than before – back to his chair. He studied Kimberley soberly for a moment, but Kimberley wasn't keen on playing the game. He liked playing with the aeroplane better.

'When do you want me to resign?' Fatso said with a sigh.

'We don't,' Kimberley said, looking up with a smile. 'In fact, we want you to keep up the good work.'

'I beg your pardon?'

Kimberley stared Gerry Douglas in the eye. 'Lord Sandford is bent, Gerry. He's trading a product with Iraq. Frankly, we don't know what. Your job is simple: screw the arse off Lady Sandford and find out what's going on. Any questions?'

The above is a description of a chain of events that could lead to an international crisis. Indeed, a high level political crisis, the type of thing Frederick Forsyth has made popular in his novels over the past 30 years.

But Forsyth doesn't just use real-life locations and security procedures, he incorporates so much more.

Forsyth was the creator of the Documentary Thriller. A story neatly wrapped around real-life events as diverse as the end of the Cold War, *The Deceiver* (1991), or the Gulf War, *The Fist of God* (1994). A skill now called Faction.

Forsyth explained how this trick is used in the engrossing Preface to his novel *The Phantom of Manhattan* (1999): 'An author *can* start a story "cold", seemingly recounting true history but without saying so, leaving the reader guessing as to whether what he is reading truly happened or not.'

Forsyth plays this trick with all the precision of a card sharp structuring his sting; but lest we forget, he was one of the first to do this in a 'current affairs' type way, bringing in real-life characters – politicians – some of whom were still in power when he released his thrillers (e.g. Margaret Thatcher): '(that) blend of truth and invention now called "faction"', Forsyth writes in the Preface to *The Phantom of Manhattan*. But how does he get away with it? He explains: 'A useful ploy in this methodology is to intersperse the fiction with genuinely true interludes that the reader can either recall or check out. Then the puzzlement in the reader's mind deepens but the author remains innocent of an outright lie.' This last line is most important, as it explains how Forsyth protects himself against libel. He only mentions *real* people briefly, in their natural surroundings, or in a factual – well-documented – incident; as he again qualified in *The Phantom of Manhattan* Preface: 'But there is a golden rule: everything you say must be provably true or completely unprovable either way.'

It is truly from this bulb of opportunity that Frederick Forsyth's fiction has blossomed.

It may seem a very novel idea now, but to Frederick Forsyth it seemed the most natural thing to do. At the time of writing his first novel *The Day of the Jackal* (1971) in 1970, he was an established journalist, having worked for both Reuters and the BBC. Also, as a journalist, he had published *The Biafra Story* (1969), a 'controversial' interpretation of the frustrations in this Nigerian province in the late 60s.

The Biafra Story was essentially a reportage of what Forsyth witnessed first hand while working there for the BBC and later as a freelancer. It would be – for the time being – the culmination of his work as a journalist.

Then came *The Day of the Jackal*. But how did this novel follow on from *The Biafra Story*? What was the connection?

It was essentially artistic progress. Forsyth just fancied writing a novel. As he was a journalist, keen to tell the facts of a story straight, he decided to do the same in novel form, writing about a movement called the Secret Army Organisation (OAS) who, in the early 60s, set out to assassinate President Charles de Gaulle. Forsyth reported the facts about the OAS as the basis of his story – early in Chapter One – then he created a well-thought-out and stimulating chase novel set around Europe, with the French and British governments working together to kill the Jackal before he killed the President of France. The story was as basic as that.

Over the years, Forsyth's work has become more intricate; but books like *The Day of the Jackal* (1971) and *The Odessa File* (1972) remain two of his most simple but memorable works. It could be said that, from the early 70s, Forsyth has worked his way up to Grand Master level with his intricate stories; but let us not forget that progress was slow in the early days, not just with his first two novels, but also with *The Dogs of War* (1974) and to a certain extent his novella, *The Shepherd* (1975). To begin with, there was something of the early Alistair MacLean about him, as far as out-and-out boys-own adventure was concerned. This could also be somebody's – albeit wrong – interpretation after reading the Prologue to *The Devil's Alternative* (1979); but it was this book that paved the way for such brilliant thrillers as *The Fourth Protocol* (1984), *The Fist of God* (1994) and *Icon* (1996), some of his most important work.

After his first three novels had become bestsellers, the die had been cast: the professional journalist had become an international bestselling novelist and, although surprised, he liked the idea, especially the money, as he had been close to the breadline while writing *The Day of the Jackal*.

But where did this man come from? Where was he born? Where did he acquire the knowledge and skill to write such intricate fiction? Who was this Jackal?

This book explores the life and work of thriller writer Frederick Forsyth. His life up to the release of *The Day of the Jackal*, and then in more detail at his novels thereafter and what makes them – and ostensibly him – tick.

It is not an exposé and consequent dissection of the man behind the work. It is a document of one man and his work and, although there are many people who feel that the whole story cannot be fully told that way, let us begin with a little eastern philosophy: 'You live, you die, so what?'

Part One
The Forsyth Story

1

The Adventurer

This is what he had wanted for a long time, from the days
when he had pressed his nose to the travel agent's windows
and gazed at the posters showing another life, another world,
far from the drudgery of the commuter train and the forms in
triplicate, the paper clips and tepid tea.

The Day of the Jackal

SOME PEOPLE long for adventure, others don't. Novelist
Ernest Hemingway spent a lifetime travelling the world,
experiencing and writing about culture and adventures others
would never dream of.

People fascinated Hemingway, rich and poor alike. He
instinctively knew the basic requirements of living and,
ostensibly, happiness: money, food, clothing, companionship,
and the various ways people appreciated or possessed these
things. Because without them people feel vulnerable, and,
sometimes, they die for want of them.

The thriller writer exploits these basic necessities as
weaknesses in 'his' novels. Money – lack of it, greed for it, just a
longing for it – becomes a motive for many crimes, from gun-
running to treachery, while the stripping of food, clothing and

friendly companionship are just the beginning of the manipulation of traitors and criminals in exposing their secrets. Indeed, all these factors expose the fundamental weaknesses of the human race, something that lies deep inside every one of us. And the thriller doesn't just expose the subtleties of this real-life flaw, it also opens the door to our own personal Room 101.

> Leonid Zaitsev, the Rabbit, was dying but he did not know it. He was in great pain. This he knew.
> Colonel Grishin believed in pain. He believed in pain as persuasion ... Zaitsev had sinned and the Colonel's orders were that he should fully comprehend the meaning of pain before he died.
>
> *Icon*

The thriller – by its very title – should be exhilarating and make us marvel. Often it shocks (see above quote). The reader is invariably left asking questions, such as: could that happen? Did that happen? And, of course, if it did happen, why weren't we – the general public – informed about it?

One of the most popular thriller writers, a man who constantly tempts the reader to ask questions, is Frederick Forsyth.

In his novels, Forsyth explores human weaknesses, mainly through the keen – methodical – procedure of government agencies, such as the Secret Intelligence Service (SIS). It is indeed through this filter of tradition and procedure that criminal activity is broken down and the passion of the hunt is heightened.

Because he has travelled the world, Forsyth writes with authority about culture, adventure and human need, blending his findings into that age-old bible that is world politics. Oceans become ponds and traitors become neighbours; and the secret agenda of every major political power becomes his playground:

By 5.15 Valeri Petrofsky was clear of Thetford and as usual was motoring sedately south down the A1088 to pick up the main road to Ipswich and home. He had been up all night and was tired. But he knew his message must have been sent by 3.30 and Moscow would know he had not let them down.

The Fourth Protocol

Forsyth wasn't born into a life of high politics or journalism. He was born the son of two shopkeepers in Ashford, Kent, on 25 August 1938. His father – Frederick – owned a fur shop in the High Street. 'Very non-politically correct,' Forsyth told me in July 2000. 'But in those days, just after the war, it was every young woman's dream to have a fur coat and I suppose people didn't really think then about all the animals that were dying to make the coat. One ought to perhaps, but they didn't. So times change.'

One gets the impression that Frederick Forsyth Snr wasn't too enamoured with his choice of profession. However, it was lucrative, as Forsyth explained: 'My father bought the fur coats from the East End. He took them down to the farmers' wives in Kent and sold them. He said, "it's a rut, but it's a fur-lined rut". And he didn't want me in that rut.'

As a young boy growing up in a rural town, Forsyth yearned for excitement – danger. He was a keen reader and the works of Hemingway, Huxley and Orwell did nothing but fuel his passion for adventure. 'I'm a fan of specific books rather than one particular writer,' Forsyth confided. '*Brave New World*, *The Seven Pillars of Wisdom*, *The Last Enemy* and *Animal Farm* rather than *Nineteen Eighty Four*.'

These novels clearly show Forsyth's young influences, with a mixture of political satire and high adventure. And it was these elements that influenced the growth of the future writer, as he explained: 'I grew up with a huge bump of curiosity. And it was curiosity about the world, not whether a certain mathematical theorem can be solved or not... I wanted to see things. I wanted to go places. I wanted to know what it was like to drive a two-seater sports car, what it was like to fly an aeroplane, what it was like to fall from an aeroplane with a parachute on my back. Places and experiences, that's what interested me.

'And all of this was because I was a small boy, from a small country town in Kent. I had parental encouragement. My father was particularly encouraging. He didn't really want me to settle in Ashford and take over the family business. Undoubtedly, most of the other shopkeepers in Ashford High Street – with sons my age – did expect and, in many cases it was fulfilled, that the son would take over the family business. My father said: "Look, you go out there. There's a huge world. I've seen a bit of it. I've planted rubber in Malaya. I've seen the Far East – fascinating. Now you go out there and discover it." Probably from the age of nine or ten I rose to that and curiosity took over.'

However, there was something else that fuelled the young Forsyth, as he explained to Judy Goodkin of *The Times* magazine in October 1996: '[My father and I] were [at a railway station] at about 7.40 a.m., and it was dotted with men dressed identically: dark suits, club ties, bowler hats, rolled copies of the *Financial Times*. They looked like penguins. "What are they doing?" I asked. My father explained that these men went to offices in London every day from the age of about 20 till they were 65. And I thought, no way, forget it. Whatever else I do, I am not going to be a penguin on a suburban railway station.'

When we compare this quote to the Jackal's thoughts in Forsyth's first novel (see quote at head of this chapter), we suddenly understand more about the young Forsyth's drive and determination.

Forsyth went to Tonbridge School and dreamed of adventure. But unlike a great many students, he was to put those dreams into action.

At 16, he would disappear from organised cross-country runs at school to attend flying lessons. He kept a scooter in an allotment shed in town. It was forbidden by the school for pupils to keep a scooter, let alone skip organised sports activities. However, keep it he did, riding up to Rochester Flying School for his lessons; as he explained to me in August 2000: 'I started flying as a 16 year old on Tiger Moths, the old open cockpit biplanes.'

It wasn't long, only a few days after his 17th birthday – the legal age – when he qualified for his private pilot's licence. However, Forsyth couldn't leave school and join the Royal Air Force straight away. 'I came out of school three months after my seventeenth birthday. I never became a prefect, or anything like that. So there was time to kill before they took me into the Royal Air Force; they didn't want to take me until I was 18. Begrudgingly, they said that they would take me at 17 and a half. But I still had three months to kill. And Dad said: "You're not lying around here. What do you want to do?" So I said that I would like to go to Spain.'

Fortunately for Forsyth, there was a clause in his scholarship (back at Tonbridge School) that said students could study abroad in their last year. Forsyth was not prepared to miss this opportunity. 'Towards the end I was desperate to leave school,' he told me. 'And my father said to me: "Look son, you pass all the exams they can throw at you and I'll get you out of there." So I said, "right, OK". And I swotted and swotted and swotted and I passed and passed and passed and I went back to him and said, "I've done that." He replied, "All right, let's get you out."'

It was only this deal that secured Forsyth's passage abroad, because, as he had already officially left school, he had to go back and plead with them to let him go, something they probably wouldn't have agreed to if he hadn't passed his exams. 'I went back to the school cap in hand and said, "Look sir, it says here that..." And they raised their eyebrows and said, "No one has ever applied for this at all." But they looked at the terms and found that there was a big stash of money in the scholarship for students to study abroad in their last year. And it had never been touched.

'So I signed on for a spring course at Granada University in Malaga, Southern Spain.'

Forsyth left for Spain in January 1956, but he wouldn't spend very long there, mainly because his rebel instincts would kick in again. Instead of concentrating on his studies, he would find a more exciting pastime: practising cape work at the local bull ring with a number of Spanish teenagers.

But why did he do this? He explained to me in July 2000, 'I haven't read Hemingway for years now; but one of his books, *Death in the Afternoon*, was about bull fighting and bull fighters. I read it as a very impressionable teenage boy and became fascinated by the whole idea of fighting this extraordinarily monstrous creature.'

News of this eventually reached his father. His mother – Phyllis – became anxious for her son, and the pair of them flew to Spain and ordered him to come home. '"You're coming home with us," my mother said. "We're not having you facing a bull. Come on." So I had to leave, but we had a quick holiday first.'

However, more excitement awaited him: 'We went to Tangiers. It was a free port then, a very loose town indeed. All sorts of oddballs left over from the Second World War. It was virtually lawless.

'There were people who imported goods that were highly taxed elsewhere. They brought the goods into the free port, transferred them to faster but smaller boats – MTBs – and raced across the Mediterranean in the middle of the night to dump them on some lonely Spanish beach where they would be met by a mule train, it was something like Romney Marsh circa 1830.

'The mule train would meet the boat and pick up perfumes, soap, stockings, all the things which were unobtainable or heavily taxed in Franco's Spain, which the population wanted. And the mule train would run inland before sunrise, so by that time, the sleek grey MTBs were racing back to Tangiers. I tried to get on one of them but was turned down.'

His parents couldn't curb his passion for adventure and were naturally concerned, but they knew what their son was like; as a small child during the Second World War he had tried to hitch a ride on a tank bound for the Normandy invasion. This was normal behaviour.

Forsyth returned to England and, at 17½ – six months early – he joined the Royal Air Force and went to Turnhill in Shropshire. 'The basic trainer there was the Provost,' he explained. 'Not the Jet Provost but the Piston Provost. I took that off when I just turned 18. I was there for nine months and then I moved to Worksop to fly Vampires for a further nine months. The Vampire was an advanced trainer, although to all intents and purposes, it was a front-line fighter with corks stuck in the gun barrels (they couldn't take the guns out because it would upset the trim and weight of the aircraft). I had my first solo flight in the Vampire 19 days before my 19th birthday and I remember it with great affection.'

Forsyth loved his flying and finally got his wings in April 1958, aged 19½, becoming the youngest pilot in the Royal Air Force at that time. But from here, his career in the RAF would be short-lived, as he explained, 'I only did my two years' National Service. There was an option to stay on but it was sign on for either six or eight years. If I did sign on, they said they would include my two years' National Service within that.'

If Forsyth had signed on, his life may have turned out quite differently; but if he was so passionate about flying, why *did* he leave the Royal Air Force?

'It was 1958, and it was becoming plain that due to the increased fire power of aircraft like the Lightning, the number of active squadrons was being reduced, as was the number of squadrons with active pilots. National Service extensions were basically going to be reduced to just shuffling papers; the priority would be given to Cranwell men. I said I would stay on if they could guarantee that I could fly Hunters, and go to an Operational Conversion Unit (from Vampires to Hunters); but as there was no guarantee and only one chance in ten of pulling that off, I said that I might as well leave.'

In his Introduction to *Great Flying Stories* (1991) – a collection of his personal favourite short stories – Forsyth described his flying career as 'blink and you miss it', which gives the impression, even after years as a bestselling novelist, that he's still disappointed that he wasn't given more incentive to stay in the Royal Air Force. He qualified this further to *MOD Focus* reporter Tracey Allen in 1985: 'My other ambition was to become a fighter pilot. I had some regrets about leaving [the RAF].'

It is clear that his love of flying wasn't just a macho boyhood fantasy; it was really the beginning of a career he had only dreamed of. Even as late as the 1990s, he confessed to 'a yearning to fly again', as he told Tracey Allen: 'Each spring I consider renewing my pilot's licence.'

Short as it was, Forsyth has never forgotten the thrill of piloting an aircraft, as he clearly illustrated in his Introduction to *Great Flying Stories*: 'I never knew one . . . who had travelled in the lonely places who did not have a proper respect for the power of the Almighty . . . [and] an awareness of the inconsequential frailty of man.'

It has been the frailty of man that has been the downfall of many characters in his novels. Travel may broaden the mind – to a certain degree – but mankind, however intelligent a beast, is always humbled by the natural splendour of mother nature. And Frederick Forsyth has always been keen to strike this balance in his novels.

In going where you have to go, and doing what you have to do, and seeing what you have to see, you dull and blunt the instrument you write with. But I would rather have it bent and dulled and know I had put it on the grindstone and hammered it into shape and put a whetstone to it, and know that I had something to write about, than to have it bright and shining and nothing to say, or smooth and well-oiled in the closet, unused.'

Ernest Hemingway
From the Preface to
The First Forty-Nine Stories

2

Heads Around Doors

If anyone were to ask me what qualities make a good journalist, I would say…first, you should always try not simply to see, to witness and to report, but to understand.'

The Phantom of Manhattan

TOWARDS THE end of his National Service, Forsyth had to find work. His credentials were, of course, good: both his schooling and National Service record. He had also travelled and become fluent in five languages (French, German, Spanish, Italian and Russian). So what would he do now in Civvy Street?

From the tender age of 13 he had made up his mind as to his eventual career; as he explained to me in August 2000: 'I remember as a small boy, standing beside my father as he read the *Daily Express*. In those days, the paper was a broadsheet with a large number of foreign correspondents all over the world. And it was owned by Lord Beaverbrook and edited by Arthur Christiansen.'

Forsyth used to stand at his father's elbow, generally at the breakfast table, and stare at the front page headlines which mentioned places such as Singapore and Montevideo. 'And I would say, "Where is Singapore, Dad? Where is Montevideo?"

And he would take me to the atlas and show me where they were.'

Once Forsyth knew where those places were, he then wanted to know what the native population looked like, what languages they spoke, what they wore. 'My father was a very patient man,' Forsyth told me. 'He used to take me to the encyclopaedia and look up Uruguay or Singapore and would go into the detail with me. And I think all that fired the ambition in me that I was going to leave this small town in Kent where I was born and raised, and go and see the world. I couldn't afford to do it, but I knew a man who could. The same man who was paying all those foreign correspondents to go around the world [laughs] – Lord Beaverbrook. He could send me.'

Forsyth laughed at his own childhood naivety, however, that laughter had a tinge of amazement in it, because he did become a foreign correspondent – and a very good one at that – although he had to work hard to achieve it.

He began to hatch a cunning plan. 'Now how do I do this? Well, first I need to become a reporter in the provinces. Then come to London and become appointed a foreign correspondent, then I can travel. And that's what I did. It took time, but that's what I did.'

From the initial ambition to travel, to eventually plotting a career to do so only took Forsyth around nine years to archive. As we have already seen, during that time, he learned to fly, passed his school exams and completed his National Service. Although it can be argued that chance may have assisted him from time to time, there is no doubting the amount of hard work he put in.

When it was time to leave the Royal Air Force and find a job, Forsyth's cunning plan to be a foreign correspondent had to be put into practice. 'I was nearing the end of my National Service in the Royal Air Force, so I went back to my home town. My father then took me to see the editor of the *Kentish Express* in

Ashford High Street, who grabbed the latest edition of the trade magazine *World Press News* (WPN) and scanned the situations vacant on the back.

'He tapped one and said, "That's a very good paper, I must say a lot better than this one." He said that because the *Kentish Express* was a weekly and he told me to get on a provincial daily.'

Provincial dailies work at a much faster pace than the weeklies, covering faster news stories. They are like the London press in miniature, in as much as they impose the same deadlines. And it is assumed that an individual learns faster when placed in one.

The newspaper Forsyth applied to was the *Eastern Daily Press*; as he explained, 'They had a vacancy for a cub reporter. And the editor of the *Kentish Express* advised me to apply for that post.'

Forsyth applied from his airbase, informing his would-be employer that he was nearing the end of his National Service. 'I got my interview and I went to Norwich in uniform. The board consisted of about five or six people. They asked me when I was leaving the Royal Air Force, and I told them the end of May [1958]. They had hoped to fill the post a little earlier but they said that they liked the cut of my jib and that they would hold it open, if I would definitely come.'

Forsyth was delighted with the offer and accepted. Once demobbed, he quickly made his way to Norwich. He was only there a month before he was posted to the newspaper's King's Lynn office in West Norfolk. He would stay there for three years. 'Well, actually it was longer,' he told me in August 2000. 'There was a trial period of three months and then the apprenticeship itself – a three-year contract. And from a newspaper's point of view it made sense, because too often they were training youngsters who, as soon as they began to pay their way in the world, they were off. They reckoned it took 18 months to train someone. And that wasn't useful to the training newspaper, because as soon as somebody learned their craft they left.'

Forsyth signed the obligatory three-year contract, but towards the end, around September/October 1961, they detected that he had itchy feet and asked him if he would renew it.

He was instantly straight with his peers and admitted that he had his sights set on greater things: Fleet Street; as he advised me in March 2000: 'The magical Fleet Street. Back then there were newspapers from top to bottom. Nowadays they are all over the place. I said to my boss, "I'm going to Fleet Street to try." He let me go and I went, walking it virtually end to end, trying to get in, but never getting past the commissionaire.'

Forsyth spent his time filling in forms and writing letters, hoping that they would be sent upstairs to the editor. 'It was the old-fashioned way,' he explained. 'It worked eventually, as old-fashioned ways tend to. I was in London for three days, walking the streets, and eventually I ended up in a pub, pretty dejected, having been rebuffed everywhere.

'I found myself on a bar stool sitting next to a complete stranger. We got talking. And he asked me what I was doing, so I told him. He asked me where I was from, and I told him that I had done three years in Norfolk. He then told me that he worked for the Press Association (PA) and there was a possibility he could get me in somewhere. "Why don't you come back and see my editor?" he said. So I said, "thank you very much"'.

Little did he realise at the time that this was his big break – although he soon found out. 'It was a hell of a break,' he explained. 'We went to his office after our pub lunch and he introduced me to a Mr Jarvis who was the PA's editor-in-chief.' Jarvis listened to Forsyth's oral CV for about 15 minutes, then, waking up, asked, 'How many languages do you speak?' Forsyth told him, whereupon he was informed that he was in the right building but on the wrong floor. He needed to go up two floors to

Reuters. Mr Jarvis then duly picked up the internal phone and secured an interview for the young reporter in Reuters.

The man who interviewed Forsyth there was Doon Campbell, the news editor of Reuters. He asked him about his education, National Service and previous experience (those three years in Norfolk) and, once satisfied with the answers, agreed to take Forsyth on three months' trial. The young reporter couldn't believe his luck. He was prepared to work his trade in London and, eventually, become a foreign correspondent; but here he was – straight away – taken on at the peak, as virtually all Reuters staff are foreign correspondents.

Forsyth wasn't sent abroad straight away; as he told me in September 2000: 'Like all trialists, I was sent to the London desk to work on restrained operations, which primarily dealt with covering special requests from abroad. Reuters provides its services abroad as well as reporting of subjects abroad. For example, there might well be a Japanese delegation in London, or there might be a special order from a Japanese news agency, and we would be asked to provide coverage far above anything the London press would be interested in. We found ourselves a small core of London-based reporters, mainly filling requirements from foreign newspapers concerning their nationals, politicians or delegates in London. And that went on for six months.'

In May 1962, Forsyth received another lucky break. The deputy head of the Paris office had been diagnosed with a heart murmur; he was deemed repatriable and came back to England for treatment. Forsyth explained to me in September 2000 how this affected him: 'This left a vacancy in the Paris office, but not as you may think at deputy-head level. Everybody was promoted up one level, which meant that there was a job going at the bottom.

'A head came around the door in the office and said, "Anyone here speak French?" So I said, "yep". And I was taken off to the

French section, where a Frenchman was asked, "Can he speak French?" So he jabbered at me in French and I jabbered back at him, and he said, "Yes he can, he's very good."'.

Forsyth quickly found himself catapulted into another world. The following night he was on a plane to Paris. 'I had been living in a bedsit,' he told me. 'The rent was payable weekly, so I could cancel that within the hour. I didn't have a car – there was no point in those days, especially in London – so my whole life fitted into two suitcases.'

Forsyth spent a year and a half in the Paris office of Reuters, during which time he saw a lot of action, as he explained to me in September 2000: 'The first year proved to be a very tumultuous time, because Charles de Gaulle was about to grant Algerian independence to the Algerians. I got there in May and he did that on 1 July. It triggered a mutiny in the army, who had been fighting for French Algeria. The Colonists coming back from the Algerian coastline were extremely angry.'

This hate-group spawned the OAS. Their task was to assassinate Charles de Gaulle and topple the French Republic.

'There was the extreme right on the one hand, and also a very powerful extreme left – Communists. Students were rioting in the streets. Now riots were very much part of the era, especially in 1968, but this was 1963. So what with the terrorism and the police response on the left and the right, it was a very effervescent society.'

The intensity on both sides was so fierce – but evenly balanced – Forsyth admits, 'Had De Gaulle been assassinated, the Republic certainly would have fallen.'

So he was plunged into this political maelstrom. And it stayed that way throughout the rest of his tour.

Obviously, it was during this time that Forsyth conceived the idea of *The Day of the Jackal*, but his life was too hectic to be writing books; as he explained: 'At that time I never thought about writing it. It was just an idea in my head. I thought the OAS obviously can't do the job themselves, so why don't they contract it out to a professional?

'Then I was suddenly summoned to the office of Mr Harold King, Reuters Bureau Chief, and he said, "Do you speak German?" And I said that I did. He was obviously very grumpy about it and said, "London are offering you East Berlin. I suppose you want to take it?" I replied, "Yes, I'm afraid I do." He then replied: "I thought you would, you bugger." Then he grinned and told me that it was a good posting.'

Indeed it was. A one-man posting. There were no colleagues in the office at all. The job was to cover East Germany, Czechoslovakia and Hungary out of the East Germany office. It was then the only accredited Western correspondent post east of the Berlin Wall. Relations didn't exist between East Germany – which was considered an outlaw state – and NATO. The Wall itself had only been up since 1961 – and this was 1963 – so it was a very fresh situation and East Germany was a complete outcast among the nations. Twenty-two Soviet divisions formed an army of occupation and a very hard line of Communism reigned. So it was into this situation that Forsyth was now plunged. 'I spent a year there,' he told me in September 2000. 'I covered that sector of Eastern Europe and it was generally thought that if the Third World War did start, the spark would probably come from Berlin. West Berlin was a frightened city; East Berlin was a very drab city. Two huge Empires; the Soviet Empire and the American Empire met. The points of their guns were feet from each other. And had somebody started something, it would have consumed the whole of Berlin and started World War Three.'

Forsyth was still only 25 years old when plunged into this situation, but was he scared? 'It was a most challenging and fascinating period. I was scared from time to time, wondering when *it* was going to happen. We all then lived under the shadow of the nuclear bomb, we knew the West had enough to wipe out the planet, the Soviet Union had enough too. They were also paranoid.'

It was the full expression of this personal paranoia which Forsyth explored in Chapter Three of his novel *The Devil's Alternative* (1979). In this book, the Soviet Union are pressurised into plotting an attack on the West because of an impending famine – caused by crop failure – that could set the country back forty years. Forsyth would coldly explain how '50,000 paratroopers would drop in over fifty locations', in order to freeze out tactical nuclear airfields in France and Germany. In his next full-length novel, *The Fourth Protocol* (1984), he would again explore the threat of Communist nuclear attack from a Soviet source.

It is clear that Forsyth was heavily influenced by what he saw and felt in East/West Germany; this probably explains why he would later write about a Nazi-like uprising, albeit from a Russian source, in his thriller *Icon* (1996):

> The Rabbit sat on his bench and wondered about the document under his shirt. He did not fully comprehend the meaning of phrases like 'total extermination' or 'utter annihilation'. The words were too long for him, but he did not think they were good words. He could not understand why Komarov should want to do that . . .
>
> *Icon*

It is important to appreciate the paranoia suffered by the Soviet Union in the 60s as, all too often, the nuclear threat was deemed to have come solely from them. The reverse did apply; hence: 22 divisions of mixed armour, mechanised infantry, engineers and artillery in East Germany. But this was not all; as Forsyth pointed out to me in September 2000, 'The Russians had rockets planted in the pine forests in East Germany pointing at the West, including Britain, of course. Relationships, after the assassination of President Kennedy in November 1963, were pretty frosty, because the feeling in America was that Lee Harvey Oswald was a Communist and therefore – in a rather simplistic way – it was all Russia's fault. Of course, the paranoia of Khrushchev, and later Brezhnev, was that the West was going to attack them and they ought to perhaps mount a pre-emptive attack on the West. Some Americans thought that they should do the same.'

The atmosphere must have been vibrant, especially for a young journalist. As Forsyth remembered, 'You could feel it in the air. There was a slight hysteria in the gaiety of West Berlin. People were living under the slogan: Eat, drink and make merry, for tomorrow you'll get blasted off the face of the earth.'

A rather hysterical – loose-moralled – West Berlin was fascinating for a young man of 25. However, the extremely dour, grey, police state on the other side of the Wall was where he lived.

'Utter contrast,' Forsyth said. 'I used to flit through Checkpoint Charlie three or four times a week. I was required to live in the East; but I was allowed to visit the West. The jollifications were in West Berlin; it wasn't much fun in East Berlin.'

East Berlin did have its own treat in store for Forsyth however. In 1964 he met a man there who would sow the seed of an idea he would later use to startling effect, as he told me in September 2000: 'John Peet was a renegade British journalist. Oddly enough, an ex-Reuters man. He had been sent by Reuters years earlier to Berlin. Unbeknown to them he was a secret Communist anyway. A bit like Kim Philby, Burgess, McLean, those sort of people. Anyway, he decided that he didn't want to return, so he formally defected. Now defections from East Germany to the West were pretty frequent, in a sense everyone walking through the streets before they built the Wall was defecting from the Communist system to a Capitalist system. After the Wall, those who escaped were defecting; but he escaped the other way. It was quite an exclusive little group that was escaping from Democracy to Despotism – Capitalism to Communism, but he was one.'

The Communist machine quickly put Peet to work on the subject he knew best – journalism. He would generate an anti-West propaganda sheet, specifically anti-West Germany. The constant theme was the presence in the West German civil service – and politics in general – of large numbers of ex-Nazis. 'Well, I think we all took it with a pinch of salt,' Forsyth told me in September 2000. 'On the other hand, I thought, right, OK I'll listen to him. So I saw him. And he was the first to tell me about this mysterious self-help organisation called the Organisation Der Ehemaligen SS-Angehörigen (Odessa). In English this means: Organisation of former members of the SS.'

Peet had said that, since 1945, the Odessa had been helping ex-Nazis – especially those wanted for war crimes – to escape. They arranged for others to stay in Germany under false names. They would erase their comrades' pasts from existing records and files. This could happen because the brotherhood was very strong, the like-minded would help each other. For example, one who had been a corporal in a concentration camp was now an archivist and he would receive a request to delete the archive concerning someone else. He wouldn't need to know that person: the fact that the instruction came from the Odessa would be enough, and he would obey. So the naughty background of 'Herr Schmidt' would vaporise. And 'Herr Schmidt' could say, 'Oh, I was just a cook in the Luftwaffe, not a Major in the SS.'

Forsyth listened to all this and it struck him as very interesting; but he wasn't going to do anything about it then and there. That would come later...

Forsyth's remit as sole correspondent for 'anything East of the wall', included Prague and Budapest. He had a big parish to handle, as he explained to me in September 2000: 'I used to have to go to the Communist meetings in Hungary and Czechoslovakia, so I got more intimate knowledge of what was going on there.'

One can imagine that the information he gathered was highly desirable to people back home in Britain, especially from a political point of view. But after a year his tour of East Germany all too soon came to an end and he found himself back in Paris for six months. This – after the relative freedom of sole correspondent in East Germany – was akin to a step backwards. He soon got bored and made a decision that was considered odd. He asked for a transfer back to London.

Nobody ever did this and indeed it raised a few eyebrows. Forsyth had his reason, which he didn't exactly share with his colleagues; as he told me in July 2000: 'The reason was quite simple really. I actually wanted to move from written journalism to radio and television journalism. I thought that that was the coming medium.'

Obviously he was right and indeed he must have seen many TV correspondents doing pieces to camera in both Paris and Berlin. ITV was very small then, so in April 1965 he came back to London to see if he could get into the BBC; as he explained: 'The Beeb was just about to open its second channel. I had access to Broadcasting House and scanned BBC notices for a reporter's job and as soon as a job came up, I was there, in front of the board. Passed. So in October 1965, I joined the BBC.'

Forsyth started out as a radio journalist but didn't spend that long at Broadcasting House. Pre-Christmas, he went to Alexandra Palace to join the TV staff of the regional news and features programme *Town and Around*. Naturally, with his passion for travelling, Forsyth wanted to go overseas again. 'It was an interesting time,' he explained. 'Channel 2 had opened. And with it the first news programme shot in colour: *News Room*

2, under the editorship of Mr Peter Woon. The programme seemed to cover all the foreign stories and that was what I wanted to get involved in. I didn't get selected for *News Room 2* but what I did see come up was a vacancy for an assistant to Diplomatic Correspondent. The old Diplomatic Correspondent had retired and his deputy had risen to take his spot. The vacancy was therefore for his deputy. As far as I was concerned diplomatic meant foreign. So I assumed that I would get into the foreign branch that way.'

Forsyth was a headstrong young man. Indeed the BBC – especially in the early days – was tightly knit. You didn't just need to know the right people, you needed to be able to drink and socialise in the right clubs as well – something Forsyth was not privileged enough to do. However, he had decided that he would get where he wanted to go by default – one way or the other.

He applied for the job and, incredibly, got it. Thus, in February 1967, he returned to Broadcasting House.

Unfortunately, Forsyth found that most of the work in his new job was analytical. He had to attend Foreign Office briefings in Whitehall and undertake analysis for radio on mainly European or North American issues. There wasn't much travelling involved.

Forsyth was beginning to think that he had made the wrong move this time; as he told me in September 2000, 'I was getting more and more frustrated. So I decided to go on holiday and with very unfortunate timing.'

Unfortunate, or maybe fortunate timing? It was indeed this holiday that changed the course of his career; as he explained, 'Bang in the middle of my holidays was the six-day war in Israel. Everyone thought at the outset that Israel was going to get destroyed. Six days later, it was complete triumph for Israel and utter disbelief all round.

'I came back to find that the story was over but almost every one of our correspondents had been on that story in some way, either in Egypt or Israel itself. Quite coincidentally, the Nigeria/Biafra War started on 7 July. So within 30 days of my arrival back from holiday, a head came around the door again – heads around doors are a big part of my life – and said, "Are you free?" and I said, "yes". This chap then said, "Well, are you free to go abroad?" The answer was "Certainly I am." Then he told me that I was going to West Africa. I said that I didn't do West Africa. And this chap said, "Oh, come on Freddie, we've got Angus MacDiarmid down in Lagos, we need a guy on the rebel side; but don't worry, it'll all be over in ten days."'

3

Hush-a-Biafra

By 30 May 1967, when Biafra seceded, not only was Nigeria neither happy nor harmonious, but it had for five previous years stumbled from crisis to crisis, and had three times already come to the verge of disintegration.

The Biafra Story
A Penguin Special

THE BIAFRA conflict was one of the most brutal the Third World has ever suffered. For the most part, the British public only saw the effect that the war had on the Biafran children. It would be the first time extreme starvation would be shown on their television screens, over 15 years before Bob Geldof (later Sir Bob Geldof) would organise a world jukebox to help a similar cause.

However, Biafra wasn't just a famine, it was a bloody war. Nigeria had to suppress the succession of its eastern province. A ferocious tribal battle ensued.

The Biafra War was the start of a long odyssey for Frederick Forsyth but it was also his coming of age.

He was sent out by the BBC on 12 July 1967. Although only meant to stay for ten days, he eventually stayed there until October, as he advised me in August 2000: 'I went into the Biafra side of things. Made certain judgements that were not popular with the Foreign Office. I was called back after three months, even though the war was still going on. I was rebuked, basically told that I had upset our headquarters in Lagos and Whitehall. And was consequently banished to Westminster to work under Peter Hardiman Scott.'

Forsyth had his own perception on Biafra and, seeing that things were going from bad to worse there, rebelled against his peers, as he explained: 'This was a war that had started the previous July and by February '68 was still going on and getting worse. Bloodshed, increasing death-toll, at a higher level than Vietnam; we were talking about Vietnam on virtually every single broadcast and newscast, although nobody ever mentioned the slaughter that was going on in Biafra. So I asked my boss at the BBC if I could go back on a limited assignment to do a progress report. I was refused on the grounds that "we are not covering that war at all". So I thought, Bugger you, *you* may not be, but I am. So that was the parting of the ways. I took one week's owed furlough. Went back privately. Saw the carnage. Returned. Resigned and flew back again. I didn't give the customary three months' notice. I wrote a letter of resignation, sent it on the Friday to arrive on the Monday and went back to the jungle on the Saturday [laughs].'

Forsyth returned to Biafra on 18 February 1968.

'I couldn't get a journalistic commission before I went. I simply didn't have the time. I went down there on an ammunition flight, from Lisbon. I knew the mercenaries were running ammunition planes from there, in a rather cranky, creaking old Super Constellation called *The Grey Ghost*, which always took off on four engines but invariably landed on three. I was perched on a crate of mortar shells in the back.

'I duly got into Biafra but was immediately arrested. These chaps were paranoid, asking lots of questions, understandably.

But eventually, I went back to see Colonel Ojukwu – the Biafran leader – and I said, "I'm awfully sorry, I've rather burnt my boats," and he howled with laughter and said, "Now you're here, you'd better stay. We don't like the BBC – we think their reporting is peculiarly biased against us. Nevertheless, stay."'

Ojukwu gave Forsyth half a bungalow and the loan of a small car, both incredibly useful to the reporter. He could now see what he wanted, return to a secure base and write his stories. However, he had nobody to write for. In September 2000, he explained to me how he combatted this discrepancy: 'I started by bombarding London. I was rejected by the *Sunday Times* – they had Frank Giles, who was very much the establishment man there. But the *Sunday Telegraph* took me up, the *Daily Express* too and the *Evening Standard*. So I began to land articles and then *Time* magazine took me up, followed by a French magazine. So I scraped a living, no more than that, which incidentally didn't matter because there was nothing to spend the money on down there anyway.'

The details of what Forsyth witnessed in Biafra and segments of his articles of the time are documented in the three separate editions of his first book *The Biafra Story* (a Penguin Special, 1969, revised, 1977; and secondary hardcover revision, Severn House, 1983). The book was written in the latter part of 1968.

Suffice to say – for this record – Forsyth saw a lot of action in Biafra; as he explained to me in September 2000: 'I was in danger of having my head blown off. But combat reporting does mean having shells landing all around you – mortars and bombs. Occasionally – if spotted – I would also be shot at. In fact, that happened all the time.'

Strangely though, Forsyth didn't really feel that he was in any real danger, other than career assassination imposed by the Establishment; as he explained: 'Biafra began to collapse in December '69. I was on the third or fourth from last plane out of there. In fact, it wasn't healthy for me to stick around. My name wasn't on the Christmas card list of the Nigerian government. They had particularly taken a dislike to me, rather than anybody else. Lots of other reporters went down and reported with horror and disgust, mainly the plight of the children, who were the principle casualties. Now they weren't dying of bullet wounds, they were dying of starvation, because of the blockade that accompanied the war. And all this was new at the time. It was probably the first time the West was exposed to this type of suffering, nowadays we have seen it until we are sick and tired, it goes on and on and never seems to get any better. Dustbowl countries and civil war countries produce these images, but it was all new then and shook people badly. And the British public wanted to help. Lagos certainly got it into their heads that I had invented all of this and that I was the centre of all their problems. And the same thing, to a degree, applied to the Wilson government. I was very much regarded as a troublesome figure, especially when I published *The Biafra Story*, which quite polemically castigated the Wilson government for its role and participation.'

In London, in December 1969, it was made perfectly clear to Forsyth that he was not going to be employed in Fleet Street (because of his stance on Biafra). He had, in his own words 'been well stitched-up'. However, he got the message pretty quickly.

'I got back Christmas week of 1969, and I got the message loud and clear by the New Year, so I thought, Right OK, I'll have to do something else, so on 1 January 1970 I started writing *The Day of the Jackal*.

'On its original appearance (the book) was roundly condemned in certain areas and by certain circles. All those who condemned it had one thing in common: they were all in positions of power and authority, to wit, the establishment. That, to me, is its own commendation.

4
Winter of Discontent?

'To all press reporters'
dedication to *The Odessa File*

AS 1970 dawned Frederick Forsyth's glittering career as a journalist had ended in disaster. His stance on Biafra may have been totally correct – as the drive and delivery of his work had had a huge effect on the public – but the powers-that-be didn't like that.

If we analyse the path Forsyth's life took after leaving Reuters, we can detect a rather slippery slope. His agreement to go to Nigeria in the first place was by his own admission a step into the unknown – 'I don't do West Africa.' He was then called back and told that he wouldn't be allowed to cover any more overseas assignments and, from that, he should have seen the power of the political beast he was up against. He either failed to, or more probably, chose to ignore it. He had his own perceptions which, wrongly or rightly, were unpopular with his peers, but he would make those perceptions known. So, he returned to Biafra, where he witnessed more. On his return to the UK, he resigned from the BBC. He then went back to Biafra again. He wrote *The Biafra Story* then, eventually, returned to nothing.

In 1978, the first anthology of Forsyth's novels – *The Novels of Frederick Forsyth* (Hutchinson, 1978) – was released. For this book the author wrote a special Introduction in which he stated, 'I would like to count myself as a professional (once) in the matter of flying aeroplanes and as a reporter; as a novelist I seem destined to remain a quite damnably lucky amateur.'

He requalified this statement to me in July 2000: 'I consider myself a journalist. If you asked me to give a lecture on how to write a novel – and I'm often asked to attend book fairs and workshops – I couldn't. I know perfectly well that this is regarded as churlishness by the organisers of these festivials, but I don't lecture for one good reason. If you asked me to give a 60-minute lecture on how to write a novel I wouldn't last five minutes. I really haven't got a clue. I know about putting words down on paper but that is it...In a way, writing a book is an extended article to me.'

The irony is, that Frederick Forsyth was only reinstated as a journalist after the success of *The Day of the Jackal*. And the power of his journalistic talents has always been the driving force in his novels, as he told me in March 2000: 'Without 12 years in journalism, I wouldn't have known where to begin.'

Part Two
The Forsyth Novels

5

The Mysterious Jackal

It is cold at six-forty in the morning of a March day in Paris, and seems even colder when a man is about to be executed by firing squad.

The Day of the Jackal

JANUARY 1970 was cold and bleak. But not content to sit back and wait for something to happen, Forsyth decided to set himself the task of writing a novel. He borrowed a friend's table and started writing 12 pages of typescript a day. 35 days later – with little outside influence to distract him – he had completed his first novel, *The Day of the Jackal*.

It is clear that Forsyth had two specific ideas for a potential novel – the OAS hiring an assassin to kill Charles de Gaulle and the workings of the Odessa. Both these ideas had been knocking around in his head for a few years, based upon his time working for Reuters in Paris and Berlin.

Being a methodical sort of man, he would take the ideas – in the order that they occurred to him – as the basis of his first two novels (when he contemplated his third novel, he naturally looked at his experiences during the Biafra War and wrote about mercenaries hence *The Dogs of War*).

Because Forsyth made the decision to write his first novel so soon after his return from Biafra, one gets the feeling that he had planned to do so on the way back from West Africa. 'I've met people who said to me that I mentioned the idea of *The Day of the Jackal* to them in the summer of '69. I can't remember that,' Forsyth told me in September 2000. 'I may have. I suppose that sometime around the second half of '69, the thought occurred to me that the Biafra War wasn't going to go on for ever and it would end. I would then find myself back in London. When I did, I knew that I should write that story I dreamed up in Paris all those years ago.'

But it was still little more than a half-page idea even then, as he explained, 'Just a basic notion: to invent a character who is a very dangerous international assassin, and have him hired by the OAS to do the job of killing Charles de Gaulle, then describe how he went about it.'

Simplicity was the watchword of *The Day of the Jackal*. It was a chase novel. However, what separated it from other thrillers can be broken down into three distinct areas. 'At the time I didn't think that what I was doing was particularly innovative,' Forsyth told me. 'I didn't think, oh, I'm going to do something different. However, since then, it has been pointed out to me that I did three things and I did them through gut instinct, not through planning or calculations. First, you can't write a book where the "hero" has no name. Second, you can't write a book where real characters appear (such as De Gaulle) and have them interact with fictional characters. Third, no one had previously explained in technical detail how things happen and why they happen. For example, how you can make specialist guns, obtain forged passports, how you hire the services of an armourer. The technical details in the book seemed to take people by surprise.'

This is a very important point because by explaining the detail of how the Jackal constructed his assassination plot – down to the last detail – didn't just make *The Day of the Jackal* a competent thriller, it also made Forsyth a very streetwise and powerful novelist.

Unlike many of his predecessors – such as Graham Greene – Forsyth didn't shy away from the procedures followed by government departments, such as MI5 and MI6. Greene did, as he openly admitted at the outset of his novel *The Human Factor* (1978): 'A novel based on life in any secret service must necessarily contain a large element of fantasy, for a realistic description would almost certainly infringe some clause or other in some Official Secrets Act.'

This observation is no criticism of Graham Greene. His stories are great, but Forsyth's work does penetrate deeper into government organisations, exposing inner mechanisms and identifying real-life individuals who have played an active role in real-life scenarios.

The Day of the Jackal was rough-and-ready and the reader became totally absorbed in the plot, gladly being led by the hand into the dark world of the hired assassin: Do you want to know how to assassinate the President of France? Well, step this way and I'll show you; then you too can experience the thrill of the chase.

30 years after Forsyth wrote *The Day of the Jackal*, I asked him if it would be possible – with present-day technology at airports and road checkpoints – for the Jackal to plot his 'hit' in the same way now; bearing in mind that the novel is set in the early 60s?

'Probably not,' Forsyth said initially, then he went through the detail. 'Airports in the early 60s were free of scanners. The arches you now have to walk through, the tubes you have to shove your hand-baggage down, all that came with Arab terrorism in the late 60s. Basically, the Jackal acquired a rifle from Genoa, and he put it in a series of aluminium tubes, which he lashed to the undercarriage of a second-hand 1962 Alfa Romeo. He then drove it from there through the Ventimiglia crossing point into France and he could still do that today. Spot-checks on cars at that crossing – from Italy to France – were a lot more thorough in the 60s than they are now. We have an open Europe now and security personnel are not looking for bits of metal lashed to the undercarriage of a car. So, to some extent, the Jackal could still get through.'

One of the most striking things about *The Day of the Jackal*, is that it doesn't have a hero. The Jackal is the main character but he certainly is no saint.

Claude Lebel, the man assigned by the French government to find the would-be assassin, is the closest we get to a genuine hero. However, this man, despite his talents as a detective, is ruled by his wife, Amélie. Once the case is assigned to him, his first thoughts are what his wife's reaction will be:

> But because he was what he was, he thought of none of these things. He was puzzling as to how he would explain over the phone to Amélie that he was not coming home until further notice.
>
> *The Day of the Jackal*

Lebel's reaction is hardly that of a courageous man, however the contradiction is that Lebel does act courageously towards the end of the book...

The characters in *The Day of the Jackal* are fascinating rather than endearing. This is because their actions are an intricate part of the fast moving story. This – in itself – gives the book an added smoothness, as there are no redundant paragraphs filled with inessential character histories, analysis or actions. All the characters exist solely to do their jobs, and to do them well:

Claude Lebel was back in his office at nine o'clock, to find a message asking him to ring Commissaire Valentin at the commissariat in Tulle. He was through in five minutes. While Valentin talked, he took notes.

The Day of the Jackal

If Forsyth thought that he was going to make an instant fortune from *The Day of the Jackal* he was very much mistaken. Two things he initially didn't know was that it was a 100/1 shot of his first novel ever getting published in the first place and then 1,000/1 that it would ever make any money.

'I didn't know,' he told me in July 2000. 'I was that naïve. I also thought you sold a manuscript the same way you sold a dozen eggs, for a single sum. I didn't know anything about royalties. So I wrote my first novel to get me over the hump of 1970, that was until editors commissioned me – as a journalist – to cover foreign assignments again. Unfortunately, that never happened.'

From February 1970, Forsyth attempted to sell his manuscript, but he found this to be a much harder task than he initially thought. 'I hawked that manuscript around London from February to September,' he told me in September 2000. 'It went through four publishers' hands before arriving at Hutchinson. Mr Harold Harris – a great guy – was the editorial director of Hutchinson at that time, and he was the first to read it and give it a chance, rather than just read Chapter One and reject it. He realised that it wasn't a book about De Gaulle getting killed – how could it be? He was still alive – it was a book about how *close* he came to assassination, and how the Jackal avoided all the traps and pitfalls and got through all the security until he was only a few yards away from De Gaulle – then missed.'

So Harold Harris agreed to publish the book, as Forsyth explained, '"We are prepared to publish this," he said. Then he continued, "I'll go further. I've persuaded my board to sign you up for a three-novel contract," this meant *'Jackal* plus two. He then asked me if I had any more ideas. Obviously, I was so destitute I said, "Me? Ideas? Oh, absolutely, I'm simply coming down with ideas." "Good," he said. "Write them down in synopsis form on one side of a single sheet of A4 paper and let me have them." So that's what I did.'

As I have already mentioned, these ideas were the basic storylines for his second and third novels *The Odessa File* and *The Dogs of War*. But before we move on to discuss these books in greater detail, let us explode a few myths surrounding *The Day of the Jackal*.

If we've believed the general publicity blurb over the years, it may be thought that Forsyth's first novel was an instant bestseller. In fact, this is far from the truth, as he explained to me in March 2000: *'Jackal* was released with no publicity and no review. It wasn't an instant success. What you read about it is untrue. It went *slowly* up the ratings, and it did this through word of mouth. Somebody read it and told their friends.'

This was obviously a painfully frustrating problem for Forsyth at the time. A £500 advance and a slow burning ten per cent royalty did little to ease his poor finances. But, as he still had no freelance journalism work, he had to bite the bullet and turn his hand to the only avenue open to him: writing novels. The rest – in that respect – is history.

However, there is one other common mistake people make when discussing *The Day of the Jackal*, and that is the facts surrounding the assassin's real-life counterpart: Illich Ramirez Sanchez aka Carlos The Jackal. 'There was an assassin nicknamed the Jackal,' Forsyth told me in September 2000. 'But this was in 1975. He had a shoot-out in Paris and killed three people.

'It was then discovered that he lived in Bayswater, prior to moving to France and it was the British press that labelled him Carlos the Jackal. And to this day, I am told, that I based my character on him. But it was the other way around.'

However, Forsyth isn't too bothered by this misconception, as he explained to me during the same interview. 'It amused me that the press labelled him the Jackal. Basically, the only reason was the flat that he had occupied was taken over by a subsequent tenant, and it was he who found a bag full of weapons and explosives under the bed. He promptly reported this to the police who arrived in force, and later a reporter talked his way into the flat and saw a copy of *The Day of the Jackal* on a bookshelf. It didn't belong to Carlos, it belonged to the subsequent tenant, so the reporter put two and two together, came up with five, hence the nickname was given and there it sticks to this day.'

> Although the English killer did not know it, French security experts who had through American courtesy been given an opportunity to study the precautions taken to guard the life of President Kennedy had returned somewhat disdainful on those precautions as exercised by the American secret service. The French experts' rejection of the American methods was later justified when in November 1963 John Kennedy was killed in Dallas by a half-crazed and security-slack amateur while Charles de Gaulle lived on, to retire in peace and eventually die in his own home.
>
> *The Day of the Jackal*

Instead of writing about a fictional assassination, why didn't Forsyth write about a real-life one: that of President Kennedy? He explained to me why not, in September 2000: 'From the moment it happened, through the Warren Commission, there was so much speculation. You would need a whole library of speculative books. Was the assassination pulled off by Lee

Harvey Oswald acting alone? If so, why was he obsessed with Kennedy? And then, Oswald only survived a few hours before he was killed by Ruby. And what about the idea of a second gunman and, the intriguing question: who was that man on the grassy knoll?'

Who indeed, but didn't that question appeal to his imagination?

'No, not really. I just thought, This is beyond fiction. I couldn't invent anything weirder than what happened in Dallas that day – and presumably before – because it was obviously a put-up job.

'You see, by the time I had started writing, the whole Kennedy thing had been done; there were already about a dozen books out on the subject and I didn't want to add to that and go over the same ground.'

In a way, a book about a fictitious assassination attempt on another public figure became a more 'plausible' and interesting concept.

There is a message there for any aspiring author.

Everyone seems to remember with great clarity what they were doing on November 22nd, 1963, at the precise moment they heard President Kennedy was dead.

The Odessa File

6

Hunting Nazi War Criminals

It is probably accurate to say that if Miller had not had his radio on that night he would not have pulled into the side of the road for half an hour. He would not have seen the ambulance nor heard of Solomon Tauber or Eduard Roschmann, and forty months later the republic of Israel would probably have ceased to exist.

The Odessa File

FORSYTH'S SECOND novel *The Odessa File* was released in 1972. He stated in the Foreword: 'The Odessa of the title is neither the city in southern Russia nor the small town in America. It is a word composed of six initial letters, which in German stand for "Organisation Der Ehemaligen SS-Anhörigen". In English this means "Organisation of Former members of the SS".'

The File itself was a fictional document detailing Nazi war criminals who had escaped prosecution for their crimes by obtaining new identities under the umbrella of the organisation.

Like the story of *The Day of the Jackal*, *The Odessa File* turns into a manhunt but, in this case not for a politician, but an ex-Nazi: Eduard Roschmann. So unlike *The Day of the Jackal*, we have a hero – a reporter – who tracks down a bad guy; rather than a bad guy hunting a politician.

The pace of *The Odessa File* is swift – not unlike *The Day of the Jackal* – as journalist Peter Miller tracks down his Nazi. But why is Miller so keen to do this? He only heard of Eduard Roschmann through the diary of an old Jew – Solomon Tauber – who gassed himself in his flat the day President Kennedy was assassinated. The diary was loaned to Miller by a police friend who thought the contents would make a good human interest story; but there was something else. A hidden agenda. And this is what makes *The Odessa File* such a riveting page turner. Miller's tenacity leads him to the Odessa File itself and, consequently, Eduard Roschmann, but what gave him that spur?

Peter Miller put the diary down and lay back in his chair for a long time, staring at the ceiling and smoking.

The Odessa File

Was the character Peter Miller semi-autobiographical (because he was a journalist)? After some initial thought, Forsyth told me in September 2000 that, strictly, no he wasn't. 'I think what I was trying to say back then was: at the start of the Cold War, the German generation that had taken part in the Second World War kind of blanked out what had happened, and it stayed blanked out for roughly 20 years. Obviously, today we have Holocaust memorials all over Germany, so there is now a complete admission by the German people for what happened, but that wasn't always so. In the mid-60s – when I was there – for young West German children growing up, it was an unspeakable subject, and I thought Miller would be like that. He would be in his mid-20s – as I was – in 1963, therefore he was born about 1938/39 and he was seven or eight when the war ended. So he would have been raised to the concept of total ignorance concerning the Holocaust.' Indeed Forsyth highlights this fact in his novel:

It had been difficult to find out what the teachers had meant in the immediate post-war period. There was nobody to ask, nobody who wanted to talk, not the teachers, not the parents. Only with coming manhood had he been able to read a little about it, and although what he read disgusted him, he could not feel it concerned him. It was another time, another place, a long way away.

The Odessa File

'In German school books, the whole of the Second World War was about five lines,' Forsyth explained. 'Some war to be covered so superficially. No mention of the camps, like Auschwitz, Treblinka, Ravensbrück, Belzac, Bergen-Belsen.'

This latter statement is painfully true. However, in his memoirs, Field Marshal Montgomery explained how – directly after the war – he had met a 19-year-old boy from the Waffen SS whose parents were Nazis and had committed suicide when the war was over. However, the boy decided not to flee Germany, but to stay, whereupon he was arrested and questioned by the allies. It was here that he started building a new life for himself. It would be the first time he would hear the arguments against National Socialism and, incredibly – to him – they did make sense. He began to go to church, the first time he had ever done such a thing (as his parents were opposed to it) but he believed he could find solace there and begged for a second chance in life.

So there was also a sense of shame hanging over the German people in the 1960s, people who were teenagers at the end of the war, but didn't speak of the atrocities. All this added to the total ignorance of younger Germans.

All of this is highly relevant information because if Peter Miller was brought up in ignorance how would he learn of the atrocities? Yes, he had read a little bit about the Holocaust but not enough to get as involved as he did; he needed something else, as

Forsyth explained, 'If Miller was going to start hunting a man of his father's generation, he would have to have some spur, he would have to have his eyes opened. That is why I invented Solomon Tauber's diary, to give Peter Miller his trigger, then I would show the endless rebuffs he went up against.'

> For a further twenty pages of typescript Tauber's diary described the struggle to survive in Kaiserwald concentration camp against the onslaught of starvation, disease, overwork and the brutality of the camp guards.
>
> *The Odessa File*

Forsyth did a great amount of research for *The Odessa File* as he explained: 'I started by asking myself the question: who helped certain prominent Nazis to disappear at the end of the Second World War? From this, I then found a can of worms that went on and on and on.

'Second, I looked at the on-going frustration of anti-Nazi detective work in post-war Germany. Through this, I discovered the reverse – the Odessa – and the level of protection ex-Nazis were receiving from inside West Germany long after the war. For example, an ex-colleague in a position of authority suddenly becomes aware of an investigation into their ex-sergeant, so they tip him off.'

Peter Miller's research in tracking down Eduard Roschmann emanated Forsyth's own, as he told me in September 2000: 'Peter Miller went through many rebuffs, as I did. The General State Atorney's Office in Hamburg rebuffed him – as it rebuffed me – and so on all down the chain, until again – like me – he ended up meeting Simon Wiesenthal, who started to reveal the level of corruption in the German police force and government. That's the level of cover-up there was attached to the tracing and capture of ex-Nazis.

'For example, there were young detectives, too young to have been in the war, who stumbled across something, investigated it and then suddenly drew a blank and incredibly found that their careers had ended. There was hostility, antagonism, all those sorts of things. Threats if they went back to their work. And all this happened in the early 60s, 18 years after the war had ended.'

Forsyth put Simon Wiesenthal into the story, as he explained: 'So this question of the disappearance of Nazis intrigued me. I remembered the discovery of Eichmann in Buenos Aires in 1960. Now that was specifically an Israeli operation but the info' for that came from Simon Wiesenthal. He virtually tracked the man down to Argentina, where he was living under a pseudonym. So I borrowed a little bit off that for the book, then put Wiesenthal himself in the story. So I thought of a vanished Nazi, who was seriously unlikeable, with someone on his trail (Peter Miller), and this would be a way of exposing the Odessa.'

Aside from John Peet's propaganda newspaper (see Chapter Two), Forsyth learned of the Odessa in a series of newspaper articles written by a British journalist called Walter Terry. Forsyth didn't uncover the organisation, as he explained: 'I think that that is where I started to take the Odessa quite seriously; this wasn't John Peet's pro-Communist propaganda, this was something far more tangible.'

However, the important point with *The Odessa File* is how it led to the arrest of a real-life Nazi, Eduard Roschmann, as Forsyth explained: 'Roschmann wasn't fictional. He existed. He was The Butcher of Riga. And he was discovered in Argentina after the release of the film of my book in 1974. One of his neighbours went to see the film. Sat there. Stared at the screen and said to himself: "He lives down my street." So he denounced him to the Argentinian authorities – which just happened to be during a brief window of democracy between the regime of two generals – Roschmann was then arrested by the Argentinians who, informed the West German Embassy who consulted Bonn. They immediately issued a writ for extradition, which went back to Argentina. Roschmann then appeared before a magistrate's court. The magistrate was sympathetic to him and bailed him. So he was on bail awaiting a final decision. But he lost his bottle, believing that he would eventually be extradited back. He didn't want to go. So he ran for the northern border, to Paraguay, which was a totally safe area. (Paraguay was a near-Nazi state, which sheltered a great many ex-SS men.)

'However, Roschmann had a massive coronary on the ferry, in the middle of the river separating Argentina and Paraguay, so when it landed on the other side, it was carrying a dead body. When they laid him out on the slab and looked at his papers the Argentinians said to the Paraguay officials, "He's in your territory, we don't want anything to do with him."

'Two inspectors from Vienna went out to ID the body and they brought back his photo and fingerprints, but also something else. A copy of my book, *The Odessa File*. And this was the clincher in identifying the body as Roschmann, as the book mentioned Roschmann's two missing toes on the left foot, which he had lost by frostbite when escaping from a train in the high Austrian Alps in the mid-winter of 1947.

'So Roschmann was buried in an unmarked grave. And there he lies to this day.'

Sometimes the condemned men would pray to the Lord, sometimes they would cry for mercy. Roschmann liked to hear this. He would pretend he was slightly deaf, cocking an ear and asking, 'Can you speak up a little. What was that you said?'... Within a few months Eduard Roschmann had become the Devil incarnate to us prisoners.

The Odessa File

The other Nazi Forsyth exposed – or really mentioned in *The Odessa File* – was General Streckenbach, who was one of the last full ranking generals of the SS and had won the iron cross with oakleaves. Forsyth took up the story: 'Now he had remained univestigated and unexposed since the end of the war. I discovered that he was a retired insurance salesman in Hamburg. So I thought, Bugger this and shoved him into the book as well. The German equivalent of PC Plod then went around to arrest him, but Streckenbach was bailed.' Streckenbach died in Hamburg in 1977.

All of this is quite extraordinary research material, especially for what was essentially a work of fiction, but how did Forsyth carry out his own research and expose these people? He explained to me in November 1999, with regard to General Bruno Streckenbach: 'I went through the list of unaccounted for senior officers. However, some of the foulest Nazis were those of quite low rank – 2nd lieutenants and sergeants, these were the ranks that ran gas chambers – but, obviously, the men responsible were the senior officers, and there were very few unaccounted for, but there was this one – Bruno Streckenbach. So I discovered that he was in the country and it was unlikely that there were two people in the country with the same name – especially at the right age – so I bunged him into the book. He didn't play any role in the book – I just bunged him in for the hell of it.'

'Take, for example the man mentioned in Tauber's diary and by me just now, Gestapo chief and SS-General Bruno Streckenbach. Remember the name?'

'Of course,' said Miller. 'What about him?'

'Walking around Hamburg, free as air,' said Wiesenthal.

Miller looked stunned.

The Odessa File

'There was one other thing about *The Odessa File*,' Forsyth told me. 'And this came years later. I discovered that the Nazis – especially the SS – had their own private pool of gold, which was separate from the Reichbank. It was mainly gold from the teeth of Jews slaughtered in the concentration camps, which had been melted down and made into ingots. And the Nazis had a dream. They knew, certainly by the winter of '44, that they were going to lose the war, so they devised a dream which was the resuscitation of the Third Reich – a Fourth Reich – which would need funding. They spirited all the gold away to Zurich, planting it in a vault under the streets of that fine city. I discovered this and put it in the book. For 25 years nobody did anything about it, then, about four years ago, the Jewish World Congress discovered this message in my book, started their own enquiries, and Lord Janner (House of Lords) began to make enquiries too, and between them they managed to squeeze a billion pounds out of the banks of Zurich. All this through a book – by then – 25 years old.'

Although Forsyth was proud of this discovery, he wasn't content with it, as he told me: 'Had I but known how important this small piece of information was – I slipped it into my book almost as an afterthought – I would have given it a whole chapter. I didn't: I gave it about 30 lines, which wasn't enough. I should have realised how important that tip was, because in 1971, it was only about 25 years after the war ended; men who had been part and parcel of that operation would only probably be in their late 50s, now they're all probably dead or, at least, in their 80s. So I should have seen the extraordinary story I had been given. It was one of the big stories of my life and I missed it, and by pure stupidity.'

For clarity's sake: in January 2001, Lord Janner QC, who is Honorary Secretary of the All-Party Parliamentary War Crimes Group and was himself a War Crimes Investigator in the British

Army of the Rhine, told me, '*The Odessa File* did not start the process of the recovery of Nazi gold from Swiss banks, but it made a vast contribution to its success. After 50 years, documents became available in the US Government Archives in Washington DC and were researched by World Jewish Congress. One of them made it clear that Britain knew that Nazi Germany passed gold, stolen from occupied countries and torn from the teeth of concentration camp victims, through to Swiss banks. This gold fuelled both the Nazi war effort and the concentration camps. The then Foreign Secretary, Malcolm Rifkind, denied that British authorities knew of this gold transfer. I produced the letter sent to me by World Jewish Congress, showing he was wrong. Honourably and immediately, he set up an enquiry, which reported swiftly and showed the complicity of the Swiss, beyond doubt.

'I then asked Rifkind to agree to convene a Conference on Nazi Gold, bringing together all nations who had been involved in the gold scandal, either as recipients or as victims. He refused. But Labour's Shadow Foreign Secretary, Robin Cook, agreed that if our Party was elected, he would convene that Conference – and two weeks after our 1997 victory, he announced that he was keeping his word.

'It was at that stage that we read again *The Odessa File*, that brilliantly researched and gripping novel in which Frederick Forsyth presents the truth as fiction. It was that truth that ever since we have worked to extend and to form one basis for restitution and at least a measure of compensation for some of the survivors of the Holocaust – Jews and gypsies, political prisoners, slave labourers, gays... and, as Forsyth points out in *The Odessa File*, "close to 200,000 non-Jewish Germans and Austrians – either mentally or physically handicapped unfortunates or so-called enemies of the Reich, like Communists, Social Democrats, Liberals, editors, reporters and priests, who spoke out too inconveniently, men of conscience and courage, and later army officers suspected of lack of loyalty to Hitler". We owe much to Frederick Forsyth's research and revelations.'

Despite this, Forsyth still feels that he should have given more space to the missing gold in his novel, as he told me, 'The big story was the missing gold, and I only really dealt with that superficially.'

To be fair to the book, on the second page of the author's Foreword, Forsyth stated: '...vast sums of SS gold were smuggled out and deposited in numbered bank accounts...' So the hiding of the gold was mentioned quite early in the book – it wasn't hidden within the story – as I pointed out to him. However, Forsyth replied, 'Yes, but it's like being told that there has just been a shooting in downtown Dallas. You're there and it's 22 November 1963, and you say, "OK" and order another beer.'

So on the basis of this comment, could we say that *The Odessa File* failed to deliver its various messages in time for someone to do something positive with them? No. *The Odessa File* achieved so much – in the real world – albeit not very quickly, but it did eventually make a difference, and that is the important thing.

Forsyth freely admits that the book was written flat out in about 25 days. A hell of a book to write so quickly and, perhaps, that is where his guilt regarding *The Odessa File* stems from: if he had taken as much time over writing it as researching it, he might have made the book's messages clearer.

It would be agreeable if things in this world always finished with all the ends neatly tied up. This is very seldom the case.

The Odessa File

7

Unleashing *The Dogs of War*

As he stared a small germ of an idea began to form in his mind. Another man would have laughed and dismissed it out of hand. Sir James Manson was not another man. He was a twentieth-century pirate and proud of it.

The Dogs of War

WITH FORSYTH's third novel *The Dogs of War*, he took the imagery from his experiences during the Biafra War to create his story, as he explained to me in September 2000: 'After I had written *The Day of the Jackal* and *The Odessa File* I thought: what else do I know about? The answer was West Africa. Let's go into battle with the mercenaries, and that was how the book came about. I used the background that I had witnessed in Biafra.'

George Jesse Turner was a *World in Action* cameraman back in 1969. The week Forsyth came back from Biafra, Turner went out there, as he (Turner) told me in May 2000: 'We went to Biafra Christmas week, and it was a very crucial time, as the place was collapsing. Forsyth had spent a lot of time out there with Ojukwu and *The Dogs of War* came from that. If you read the book, all you have to do is substitute certain aspects for real-life events... I only spent 72 hours out there, got a snapshot of what happened, but he saw a lot more and put it into his book.'

It would be wrong to suggest that *The Dogs of War* was written solely about Biafra because, quite frankly, it wasn't. In February 2001, I asked Forsyth how much of the book was influenced by what he witnessed during that war. He told me: 'The first chapter only: Colonel Ojukwu's last night in Biafra. It happened exactly the way I phrased it in the book. An African pilot – called Van Cleef – put his life at risk in order to fly Ojukwu out. But he came on spec and Ojukwu said, "You're very kind, but I already have a lift from the president of the Ivory Coast." However, Van Cleef did take out some other people, as requested by Ojukwu. And that is the book's only connection with Biafra.'

The Dogs of War was another fast-paced thriller, investigating corruptions in mining, high finance and the secret world of the arms dealer. The story: Sir James Manson, the ruthless head of a London-based mining concern, is involved in a plot to overthrow the government of a remote African republic and eliminate its dictator. Manson's motives are far from unselfish, and word of his firm's mineral discoveries leak to the Russians, while 'Cat' Shannon – the leader of the mercenaries recruited by Manson – is getting together his attack force.

Step by step, Forsyth takes us through Europe – from Paris to Ostend and Marseilles, where the mercenaries are recruited; from Berne to Brugge, where the undercover financial deals are set up; from Germany to Italy, then Spain and Yugoslavia, where the arms are bought and a ship commissioned to transport the men and their equipment to a battle for the African president's palace.

The important thing to note about Forsyth's first three novels is their 'User Manual' approach. Do you want to know how to be a hired assassin? Answer: *The Day of the Jackal*. Do you want to become an investigative reporter? Answer: *The Odessa File*. Do you want to be a soldier of fortune? Answer: *The Dogs of War*.

As Forsyth mentioned when discussing *The Day of the Jackal*, people were surprised by the amount of detail he put into his books. The detail was so well researched and intricate that it added an extra fascination to an already intriguing story: 'So that's how they do it,' the reader would say. Or in regard to *The Odessa File*: so that's how an investigative reporter works. Obviously, *The Dogs of War* worked on a similar principle with regard to soldiers of fortune, starting with a factual scene from the collapse of Biafra; even the prologue includes a Super Constellation aircraft which Forsyth hitched a lift on in order to get into Biafra in the first place:

> The pilot of the DC 4 brought his plane to a halt twenty yards from the Super Constellation already parked on the apron, killed the engine and climbed down to the concrete.
>
> *The Dogs of War*

All of this is no criticism of Forsyth's novels. In fact, it goes a long way to show – once again – that meticulous research adds to the realism in a work of fiction. But where *The Dogs of War* differed from *The Day of the Jackal* and *The Odessa File* is that it was more fiction than faction. Basically, Forsyth was turning into a novelist. However, he found *The Dogs of War* hard going, as he explained to me in September 2000: 'I was late in handing *The Dogs of War* to my publisher. They wanted it in the winter of '72 but it was finished in May '73 and published in '74.'

Because he was writing and researching mercenaries, I asked him if he encountered any problems while researching them, i.e. was he ever threatened when researching that particular aspect of the book. 'No threats,' he said. 'Writers are funny in that sense, as they seem to be untouchable in that way. The Mafia have silenced a few journalists. Killed them, but it is very rare for the underworld to ostracise a journalist. Maybe they think that it will be counter-productive as there would probably be investigations made against them.

'Writers seem to be able to do things which a grass or informer would get a contract put out on them for, journalists rarely do. Now they might intimidate you, if you haven't written it yet, if they find you enquiring. I was warned off when I was researching *The Dogs of War*. I was investigating the arms trafficking going on in Hamburg. And it was discovered that I was. So I was warned off. As it happened, I had completed all that I wanted to do anyway, so they were too late. They told me to get out of Hamburg, so I got out of Hamburg, because a) I didn't want to be beaten up and b) I had got everything I wanted anyway. When I published *The Dogs of War*, there wasn't a peep from them.'

Long ago in the Congo he had seen the same attitude, the black-eyed sense of menace conveyed by an African of almost primeval cultural level, armed with a weapon, in a state of power, wholly unpredictable, with reactions to a situation that were utterly illogical, ticking away like a moving time bomb.

The Dogs of War

An impressive aspect of *The Dogs of War*, is how well Forsyth understood the African people. This perception is almost certainly a direct result of his time living in Biafra during the late 60s. Indeed we can see this perception forming in his reportage of the war, *The Biafra Story*: 'In Biafra personal success has always been regarded as meritorious; a successful man is admired and respected. There is no hereditary office or title. When a man dies his success in life, his honours, his prestige and his authority are buried with him. His sons must fend for themselves on the basis of equal competition with the other young men of the society.'

Forsyth would come to understand the West African people, their customs, their ways. So on the basis of this, it is clear that the mercenaries in *The Dogs of War* would not get away with their bloody quest. Forsyth's understanding of the people Manson and his men are up against was deep and, perhaps, a little ahead of its time for 1974, as the world, especially the British people, did not have much idea of the conflicts in West Africa – some did, others didn't. Perhaps this is the reason why *The Dogs of War* was such a riveting read in the 70s.

However, despite this, Forsyth does touch on a more negative aspect of Africa: cannibalism, as he wrote in *The Dogs of War*: 'As the priest looked he saw that the mountain seemed to be glittering in the morning sun, and he called it the Crystal Mountain. He noted this in his diary. Two days later he was clubbed and eaten. The diary was found by a patrol of colonial soldiers a year later, used as a juju by a local village.'

Forsyth has come across similar circumstances himself, as he explained to Sarah Tucker in the *Metro* (May 2001): 'Most of my worst experiences have been in Africa. Many years ago, I was in West Cameroon and contracted malaria. I had been travelling by bus with locals through the jungle and, when they realised what I'd got, they swiftly kicked me off in the middle of nowhere either to recover or rot. I crawled away into the jungle, sweating it out for six days without quinine until the fever broke. I then thought it might be a good idea to try to find a town or village, which might have a Jeep to take me to an airport. After walking for a few hours, I found a village in the jungle which seemed to be surrounded by glowing tree lights. It was quite beautiful but, as I drew closer, I realised they weren't tree lights at all – but severed heads on sticks, all in various stages of decomposition.

'The villagers started to surround me, looking me up and down. But their chief obviously wasn't hungry that day, so they let me go.'

Like all old hands, he alternately loved and hated Africa, but conceded it had got into his blood over the past quarter century, along with the malaria, the whisky and the million insect stings and bites.

The Dogs of War

The Dogs of War was a pivotal novel for Forsyth. However, the level of research and the intensity of a three-book commission had begun to take its toll on him.

After writing the novel, he decided to take a long break (at the time he had told the press he had quit), as he explained, 'I was a professional novelist by now, because I had been researching, promoting or writing three novels in 30 months (two and a half years), which is fairly heavy pressure. So I decided to do two things: one, I got married and, two, I stopped writing for five years. I married an Irish girl [Carole, in 1973] and went to live in Ireland the winter of '74, and spent '75 to '79 inclusive there.'

To put things into perspective, Forsyth decided to stop writing in the summer of 1973, got married and spent a long vacation in Spain. He then moved to Ireland to start a family and 'modernise an old Irish manor house'.

During that period, Forsyth wrote only one full-length novel, *The Devil's Alternative*, something, in retrospect, he now deems to be a little foolish, as he explained: ' I admit, I also wrote *The Shepherd*. But I gave that to my wife, so I didn't make any money on it. But the actual sale – the money from *The Devil's Alternative* – came after I left Ireland, so, foolishly, I didn't take advantage of Ireland's zero taxation for authors' rule. Everyone else assumed that I was there for that reason and that reason only. I would have been smart to write furiously during that period, but I didn't.'

Aspects of Forsyth's career as a journalist fashioned his first three books. This – almost by default – created the 'faction novel'. And through his clear and methodical style – bringing in world-wide political issues – he achieved international bestselling status. Obviously, *The Dogs of War* allowed him to become more imaginative, as far as developing plausible characters and situations not necessarily totally reliant upon real-life people or events. However, because of the intensity of that workload – and due to the fact that he had just got married – he decided to quit and become a family man. And why not, he had done enough for the time being.

8

A Christmas Ghost Story

For a brief moment, while waiting for the control tower to clear me for takeoff, I glanced out through the Perspex cockpit canopy at the surrounding German countryside. It lay white and crisp beneath the crackling December moon.

The Shepherd

DESPITE THIS sudden urge to become a family man – the marriage produced two sons, Frederick and Shane – Forsyth soon found himself writing another, quite different, story – his only novella, *The Shepherd*.

The novella was instigated by his wife, Carole, as he explained to me in March 2000: 'I wrote *The Shepherd* for my wife. She thought – wrongly – that I had forgotten to buy her a Christmas present. So she told me to write her a story. I wrote *The Shepherd* – a rather short, slim volume – in a day.'

The Shepherd is, essentially, typical of the traditional British ghost story as, like the Christmas books of Charles Dickens, it is an illustrated novella and evokes some wonderfully festive imagery:

Down there amid the gaily lit streets the carol singers would be out, knocking on holly-studded doors to sing 'Silent Night' and collect *pfennigs* for charity.

The Shepherd

However, despite the holly and obligatory spectral image, Forsyth was keen to avoid clichés; as he told me in March 2000: 'I didn't want to write a typical haunted house story with creaking banisters and such things. I did it my own way. I had to include the theme of Christmas, hence the title, and the supernatural aspect worked well with the awful loneliness of a single-seater fighter cockpit lost in the freezing vault of a winter's night with the radio gone. Also, the fog closing in, the fuel dropping and nothing beneath but the pitiless North Sea added to the imagery.'

For a second I thought it was my own shadow, but with the moon up there my own shadow would be behind me. It was another aircraft, low against the fog bank, keeping station with me through my turn, a mile down through the sky towards the fog.

The Shepherd

There are autobiographical references within the text of *The Shepherd*. To begin with, the aircraft our hero is flying is a Vampire – which Forsyth used to fly himself – also, he mentions quite early on, the pilot's original RAF training: 'The important thing, they used to say in flying school, is not to know how to fly in perfect conditions; it is to fly through an emergency and stay alive. Now the training was beginning to take effect.'

Obviously, during his brief career as a pilot, Forsyth had a few scary moments; as he explained to me in March 2000, 'There are moments when you think that you are going to die in the next ten seconds, and you haven't got the time to prepare and you say

"Oh, f—". I'm sorry to say that what we said in 1957 was a lot less printable than the *Boys Own Paper* speak of W. E. Johns. When facing imminent death, all his characters would say was, "Oh gosh." '

We can forgive this indiscretion, I'm sure. Suffice to say that there is no bad language in *The Shepherd* unless you include: 'I swore a most unseasonal sentiment against the compass and the instrument fitter who should have checked it for 100 per cent reliability.'

The Shepherd is made increasingly disturbing by the pilot's controlled panic after realising that he is in danger. That and the fact that he puts his life into the hands of his mysterious saviour who guides – shepherds – him back to earth, clearly shows another – albeit modern-day – Christmas miracle:

> Yes, it was the last attempt to save one's life. I recalled the details better now. The rescue aircraft who would lead you back to a safe landing, flying wing-tip to wing-tip, was called the 'shepherd'.

The Shepherd

Forsyth's novella is completely set at night, and, as World War II flying hero John 'Cats Eyes' Cunningham told me in November 1999, 'You are totally reliant on your radar and your instincts in those circumstances.' Indeed the pilot in *The Shepherd* is totally reliant on his instincts, perception and experience as his instruments have died on him. However – and this is a very strong image in the story – there is throughout the constant assistance from a large, bright moon (see quote at head of this chapter), which impresses itself on our imagination from the very first paragraph of the story, adding a wonderfully gothic touch.

Forsyth has a gift for exploiting clichés and turning them into powerful and relevant images. It comes down to perception. As we explored in Chapter Five, Forsyth could have written a thriller about the Kennedy assassination, but to transfer the assassination idea to another living person – an attempted murder which clearly didn't work – not only added its own scenario of realism, but blew away the cliché.

The Shepherd wasn't Forsyth's first attempt at – what is essentially – a short story. He had written a couple before, both of which would appear in his anthology of short stories *No Comebacks* (1982). The idea of latching on to an original idea and converting it into a good story very quickly, seems to be his forte (both *The Day of the Jackal* and *The Odessa File* each took a month to write respectively). The difference with *The Shepherd* was that Forsyth didn't need to do anything apart from write from experience – the research was minimal. He wrote the story in a day.

> Behind him, quite clearly visible, stood his aircraft. There were the two low-slung pods housing the twin Merlin engines that gave it its remarkable performance.
>
> *The Shepherd*

Forsyth's love of flying shines through in this rather underrated Christmas ghost story. Although his shortest single work, it speaks volumes about his love of flying and attitude towards life: constantly living on the edge in his younger days but now – the period (1975–79) – happy to live life as a family man.

The Shepherd was, in its own little way, the epitaph to Forsyth's youth.

9

When the Devil Drives

The president of the United States read the memorandum
with an expression of increasing horror.

'This is appalling,' he said when he had finished.
'Whichever option I choose, men are going to die.'

The Devil's Alternative

FORSYTH'S NEXT novel was *The Devil's Alternative*. A book
many people – both fans and reviewers alike – consider to be
his best.

As we know, *The Devil's Alternative* was the only book Forsyth
wrote during his five-year stay in Ireland. However, it would be
unfair to say that he was totally unproductive – in a literary sense
– during that time.

In 1976 Forsyth revised the text and wrote a special
introduction to the first reprint of his reportage of the Biafra War,
The Making of an African Legend: The Biafra Story. He also
wrote a short story that would later appear in his anthology *No
Comebacks*, and a special introduction to his first collected
anthology of novels, *The Novels of Frederick Forsyth*, which was
published by Hutchinson in 1978. And if that wasn't enough, he
wrote five film treatments as well.

Forsyth needed to build upon the respect and success he had won with his first three novels. *The Devil's Alternative* was the answer. It was to be his most intricate and cerebral novel to date.

It was in 1977 that he began to toy with the idea of his next novel. By the spring of 1978 he had formed the story in his head, but he was still undecided whether or not to write it in novel form as he had been writing film treatments. However, it was his wife who settled the question, as Forsyth wrote in his Author's Introduction to *Frederick Forsyth – The Four Novels* (Hutchinson, 1982): 'While aware that in my writing periods I become grievously uncompanionable, she [my wife] was also of the view that when I had a story trying to get out, I am even worse. So in April 1978 I started the series of journeys and secret meetings that were necessary to garner the factual research I needed. By mid-October I was ready, and on the 28th sat down to write, finishing on 12th December. From a phrase that had come to my attention during the researches, I called it *The Devil's Alternative*.'

But for all that, the book started very quietly, with a man adrift on the sea, dying of thirst and sunburn:

'The castaway would have been dead before sundown but for the sharp eyes of an Iranian seaman called Mario.'

This piece of luck – for the castaway – results in the unwinding of an ingenious plot that eventually builds up into an international crisis.

What is particularly satisfying about *The Devil's Alternative* is Forsyth's knack of starting major scenes with a sense of normality, almost as if we are about to witness just another day in the office: 'A gentle warming sun shone down on Washington that middle of May'. However, the problem for the president of the United States is that it isn't just going to be another day in the office; he faces a potential ecological disaster where whatever choice he makes 'men are going to die'.

The Devil's Alternative is basically the story of the hijacking of the world's biggest oil tanker and its potential to cause an ecological disaster that could pollute the whole of the North Sea.

The book was essentially built upon the international scene-hopping that Forsyth started in *The Dogs of War*, although *The Devil's Alternative* would take in the main Cold War countries (also Holland and a small country house in Ireland). Like John Le Carré, he would pull all the various locations and storylines together to create a credible and exciting thriller.

> It had been a beautiful affair, a once-in-a-lifetime love. He was twenty-four, turning twenty-five, and she was nineteen, dark and lovely. Because of her job they had had to conduct their affair in secret, furtively meeting in darkened streets... They had loved and talked, she had made him suppers and they had loved again.
>
> *The Devil's Alternative*

Among the many surprising vignettes in *The Devil's Alternative* are the secret thoughts of Adam Munro while attending a ballet. He daydreams of a clandestine assignation he once had with a girl, Valentina. Two points of interest here are: first, *The Devil's Alternative* truly presented the first whiff of a tender love scene in a Forsyth novel, but, second, and more interestingly, is that some of the actions and previous experiences of the young Adam Munro mirror the young Frederick Forsyth: a young man who works for Reuters in Berlin is then transferred to the Paris office before returning to London. A tenuous parallel, or maybe Forsyth waving a fond farewell to a past flirtation in the light of his first marriage?

Does it really matter, if it makes good reading.

> In the fourteen republics ruled by the Russian Republic are several score identifiable non-Russian nations, and the

biggest and perhaps the most nationally conscious is the
Ukraine...

The Devil's Alternative

Another point concerning *The Devil's Alternative*, is that it
doesn't focus on terrorism emanating from the far left. Quite the
reverse, it looked to the right wing. So the book doesn't directly
blame the Communist fraternity in Russia. This is an important
point, because Forsyth is not overly keen to exploit the obvious
cliché. In 1996, with the writing of *Icon*, he looked to Russia –
the biggest Capitalist country in the world – to suddenly have as
its president an extreme right-wing dictator. So, Forsyth is very
keen to ask himself the question: 'What would happen if...?'

'Yes, they hate Moscow,' replied Kaminsky. 'As much as
you or I. Their inspiration seems to be a thing called the
Jewish Defense League. They heard about it on the radio. It
seems their philosophy, like ours, is to begin to strike back;
not to take any more persecution lying down.'

The Devil's Alternative

By asking himself, 'What would happen if...?' Forsyth
constructs his intricate stories. He turns some of them around in
his mind for up to a year before thinking, 'Yes, that will work',
then researches the now formed ideas and sits down to write his
book in double-quick time, 'going into Purdah for a month', as
he puts it.

'I put it to you, sir, that destroying the *Freya* would not work.
That is, it would not solve the problem. Three days ago
Mishkin and Lazareff were two insignificant escapees and
hijackers, serving fifteen years in jail. Now they are already
celebrities. But it is assumed their freedom is being sought for

its own sake. We know different...'

The Devil's Alternative

Because of the intricacy of the plot, a novel question concerning *The Devil's Alternative* is: What was the initial idea based upon? In September 2000 Forsyth told me, '*The Devil's Alternative* is certainly the biggest and most complex book that I have ever written. But then again – like all my writing – it came from one single idea. Possibly from a magazine article, or a conversation at the dinner table.

'In those years [1970s] the western world was being constantly beset with the notion of hijacking. It was then relatively new, but the terrorists were hijacking things in Havana, Europe, in fact all over the world. They hijacked buildings like the Japanese Embassy in Stockholm. The Red Army faction was very strong, so hijacking was very common. Buildings were being hijacked, trains, aircraft, and I just thought: what's next? And then I just looked at one of those enormous oil tankers and said to myself, "You could cause utter and complete devastation, particularly if you blew up one of those in a very narrow water way like the channel, in fact, you would pollute Europe for several decades."'

So *The Devil's Alternative* grew from the terrorist epidemic of the late 70s, but how did the idea grow from there?

'Solely from the idea of a group of terrorists hijacking a huge oil tanker,' Forsyth told me. 'But I had to think: who would do it? The obvious choice was left wing, and I thought, No, let's not go there, let's go the other way – to the right. And I thought, Who are the right-wing terrorists? How about the Ukrainian Independent Fighters. An unusual group. I investigated them, found that they were very active, very passionate, very fanatical, but virtually unknown. And the idea grew and grew. For example, with the oil tanker, I thought: let's not have a small thing, let's have the world's first one million ton tanker – which was in planning at the time but still (to this day) hasn't been made – but I thought: let's have the world's first.

'I thought a million tons of Saudi Crude blown apart in the Channel would be cataclysmic, so why not hold the western world to ransom.'

Sure enough, that is what he did, and possibly because of the ecological awareness presented by this story – which is slowly turning into paranoia in the millennium – *The Devil's Alternative* continues to be one of Frederick Forsyth's most stimulating and relevant thrillers.

However, despite this, *The Devil's Alternative* proved to be the first time Forsyth would set his novel in the near future (something he would not obviously do again until *Icon* in 1996), as he explained in his Author's Introduction to *Frederick Forsyth – The Four Novels*: 'This fourth book was something of a departure, for I felt it necessary to set the action in the near future instead of the recent past. That inevitably meant hazarding a few predictions. Surprisingly, some of them have come true since the time of writing, and others appear to be not too far off. The fall of the Shah of Iran, the arrival of Britain's first woman premier, the successive Soviet wheat crop failures, the US embargo of grain shipments to Russia, the Kremlin's conquest of Afghanistan, the increasing Russian crackdown on Jews, dissidents and non-Russian nationalists, the steady splintering of the façade of the Soviet empire.' All that from just one novel.

On board the *Freya* it struck midnight. Captives and captors entered their third and last day. Before another midnight struck, Mishkin and Lazareff would be in Israel, or the *Freya* and all aboard her would be dead.

The Devil's Alternative

To this day *The Devil's Alternative* remains an intriguing and relevant novel.

10

No Comebacks

Mark Sanderson liked women. For that matter he also liked Aberdeen Angus fillet steaks, medium rare with tossed hearts-of-lettuce salad, and he consumed both with equal if passing enjoyment.

No Comebacks

FORSYTH HAD published a few short stories before trying his hand at an anthology: 'No Comebacks' (1972), 'Money With Menaces' (1973) and 'Used in Evidence' (1979). So in 1982 he decided to put together an anthology of ten short stories under the collective title *No Comebacks*, which was the title of his very first short story.

The stories all concerned themselves with such things as murder, revenge and blackmail, each having their own individual sting in the tale. Even though the stories were not as intricate as his novels, they proved that he was not short of original ideas, which was something he could quite easily have been accused of as he had not been the most prolific of novelists.

In 'There Are No Snakes in Ireland', Forsyth demonstrated that as well as writing an ingenious short story he could also write quite humorously. However, the contradiction to this is the very serious theme of racism that runs throughout:

'You ignorant darkie,' he gasped, 'don't you know? There are no snakes in Ireland. Understand? There aren't any.'

'There Are No Snakes in Ireland'

This story has been much praised for its subtleties, and it is not my intention to bore the reader by over-analysing it or the plotlines for all the stories in the anthology. However, I shall highlight a few to give the flavour of the anthology.

'There Are No Snakes in Ireland' concerns demolition workers and the frustrations between cultures. By contrast, the title story 'No Comebacks' is about a rich philanderer's plan to kill the husband of the women he loves (a story perhaps more typically Forsyth than others in the anthology).

Then we have 'The Emperor' – the third story in the anthology – and a most intriguing one. Set on the beautiful island of Mauritius, it tells the story of a hen-pecked husband and an enormous fish. I discussed this story with Forsyth in March 2000: 'I enjoy big game fishing as did the actor Lee Marvin, now sadly dead. However, novelist Wilbur Smith enjoys sea angling, so there are still a few of us about.'

Ernest Hemingway also enjoyed big game fishing and comparisons could be made between Forsyth's story 'The Emperor' and Hemingway's *The Old Man and the Sea* (or indeed Forsyth's international boys-own style of writing and that of Hemingway).

'OK, youthful passion and an abiding interest in big game fishing. I have these things in common with Hemingway,' Forsyth told me. 'I don't have his alcoholism in common, or for that matter, swaggering around France with two pearl-handled pistols.'

That may be so, but what was the driving force behind the story. He explained, '"The Emperor" was really a story about the worm that turned. A mild little man who was always put upon and thought he would settle for a life as a branch manager in a bank and then found a whole new world by pitting himself against a fish. So he suddenly found so much more to himself than anyone had ever given him credit for.'

'The Emperor' like *The Old Man and the Sea*, is a story about a man pushing himself to his physical limit – against a fish – to prove a point to himself and the people close to him.

> The Marlin had come to 300 yards when he walked again. This time the boat was in a trough and the Emperor burst the surface point straight towards them.'

'The Emperor'

The only other story I wish to comment on in the anthology is 'Duty', as it doesn't obviously fulfil the criteria of murder and intrigue. Indeed Forsyth admitted this in a footnote to the story: 'It has been pointed out to me that the following story is out of character with the others in this collection and fits into no real category. It is pure idiosyncrasy on my part, but I have decided to include it anyway. It was told to me by an Irish friend and he swore it was absolutely true and had happened to him. For this reason, unlike all the other stories, I have elected to tell it in the first person.'

Again we have that Irish connection (see 'There Are No Snakes in Ireland' and also 'Used in Evidence', the latter written before Forsyth moved to Ireland) and one can indeed imagine Forsyth sitting back to be entertained by a friend's favourite anecdote after dinner and retelling it later in his own individual way. Although a much greater departure than the other stories in the anthology, 'Duty' does leave a little pause for thought and really beggars the fact that so many uncanny vignettes occur through a person's life, a hoard of anthologies could be made from fond anecdotes alone.

After all, in those days a lot of people were executed.
Common murderers were hanged at Mountjoy. But hanged.
By prison warders. Would they need the soldiery after that?
And British soldiers would be executed too, for murder and
rape, under military regulations after court martial. Would
they be hanged or shot? I did not know.

'Duty'

In 'Duty', we can see some typical Forsyth imagery coming
through (see above quote) as far as military procedures are
concerned but this is played down somewhat. The story is
essentially about a chance meeting and the pay-off is more 'pause
for thought' than 'sting in the tail'. So in that respect, 'Duty' is a
very subtle story and completely out of context with the rest of
the anthology.

This to one side, there is always the concern that anthologies
of short fiction will not sell as well as full-length novels, however
No Comebacks sold exceptionally well, clearly showing that
Forsyth could turn his hand to yet another style of writing – the
less intricate short story. Admittedly, to some degree, he had
shown this before – with his novella *The Shepherd* – but *No
Comebacks* was a collection of quality short fiction, clearly
showing how prolific he could be in presenting original ideas to
the public.

11

A Nuclear Suitcase

The man in grey decided to take the Glen suite of diamonds at midnight. Provided they were still in the apartment safe and the occupants away.'

The Fourth Protocol

BY THE time Forsyth wrote *The Fourth Protocol*, his four previous novels and one anthology had sold a staggering 30 million copies worldwide and had been translated into two dozen languages.

On his return from Ireland at the outset of the 1980s, Forsyth took a home in London's St John's Wood. After putting together his anthology *No Comebacks* he started work on his first major novel since *The Devil's Alternative*: *The Fourth Protocol*.

Although quickly transformed into a major movie – which Forsyth had a hand in himself (see Forsyth's interview in the Film Guide in Part Three) – the novel became popular for two reasons; first, it was a thought-provoking and intricate story, and second, and more intriguingly, it hit upon the main paranoia of the 80s: nuclear disaster.

The basic story was quite simple: MI5 investigator John Preston leads a mission to prevent a Soviet agent from piecing together a nuclear device and wiping out a US air base in England. The nuclear device would be brought into the country piece by piece, via a variety of routes in an act that would breach the Fourth Protocol.

Simply, the Fourth Protocol itself anticipated that nuclear devices would one day be made small enough to fit inside a suitcase. So it banned any of the signatory nations from introducing into any national city an assembled or unassembled nuclear device for detonation (the other three protocols foresaw other potential future hazards which were not then technically possible).

> Over the years the first three protocols passed into history, either because the hazard was established to be quite impossible or because the antidote was discovered as fast as the threat became reality. But by the early eighties the Fourth Protocol, the most secret of them all, had become a living nightmare.
>
> *The Fourth Protocol*

So in Forsyth's novel, the Soviets planned to detonate a nuclear device in England and breach the Fourth Protocol, but why?

> One must be aware, of course, that there always has been a dedicated, ardently pro-Soviet Marxist-Lenninist wing deep within the Labour Party...
>
> *The Fourth Protocol*

When Forsyth wrote *The Fourth Protocol* Margaret Thatcher was in danger of losing the next general election because of the Labour Party's stance on nuclear disarmament. They were pro-disarmament, unlike the Conservative Party who have never changed their policy on Britain's nuclear deterrent.

Forsyth saw that public opinion was favouring the Labour Party's stance, so wrote a story that took this one stage further: invent a story where a US air base in Britain is blown up by a nuclear device. The public and political pressure from this would put the Labour Party in power and from there, the Marxist–Leninist faction within the party would take over. The name the Soviets gave this mission was Plan Aurora.

In a succeeding and concluding memorandum, Comrade Secretary General, I intend to show how, were that to happen, our friends of the Hard Left plan to topple Labour Party leader Neil Kinnock from the leadership in his hour of victory, and impose upon Britain her first Marxist–Leninist Premier, along with a truly revolutionary socialist legislation programme.

The Fourth Protocol

Was all this a little far-fetched? As we know – with hindsight – Margaret Thatcher did win the next election?

'No, Labour didn't win that election,' Forsyth told me in August 2000. 'Mainly because the Party was coming under internal assault at the time – known as entrism. There was a very determined minority inside Labour who, quite frankly, had in mind to take over the Labour Party.

'I believe it has ultimately been taken over, but by its ultra right wing. The ultra left wing would not have been voted into power but I created a scenario that under certain conditions the British public would vote the Labour Party into power under a moderate leader, only to have him toppled and replaced by an extremist.'

Still a far-fetched notion? Not according to Forsyth, as he went on to explain: 'With the toppling of the Labour leader, I used as my model Ken Livingstone. He was never elected leader of the Greater London Council (the GLC). A man called Mackintosh was elected leader. But in a secret late-night committee he was toppled, and the extreme Ken Livingstone became the leader of the GLC.

'Now if you can do that with the government of London, why can't you do it with the government of Britain? That became my theme for *The Fourth Protocol*, coupled with a Soviet active measure to ensure that the Labour Party would win the next election.'

In reality, did the Conservative Party win that election because of the war with Argentina?

'Yes, the Falklands factor. That was unpredictable. However, if we were defeated in the Falklands, it would most certainly have cost Margaret Thatcher the government.'

Once Forsyth had planned out his story, he had to devise a way in which British Intelligence could discover Plan Aurora. This would, in effect, start a chase novel, almost similar in format to *The Day of the Jackal*, i.e. one man has the power to carry out the execution of a political task and the authorities must thwart his plans; but first they have to find him.

So how do the authorities learn of the Soviets' Plan? Quite ingeniously. The book opens with a jewel robbery. A safe is broken into and some jewels are taken away in a bag (also contained in the safe). Unbeknown to the thief at the time, that bag also contains secret documents. However, when he does find out, he returns them to the Ministry of Defence (MOD).

He took the ten secret documents and left. Capstick was right, he thought. It's a leak, and a bad one.

The Fourth Protocol

The idea of a thief returning secret documentation to the MOD in order to protect his country is not a bizarre notion, as Forsyth explained, 'Years after I wrote *The Fourth Protocol* a similar thing happened. In the Gulf War, there was a wing commander on the planning staff who had his car stolen in West London and, on the back seat, there was a computer that contained the whole attack campaign on its software. But the thief sent back the software to the MOD. So it was similar to what I wrote in *The Fourth Protocol*: a thief returning documents to the MOD saying, whoever left this should be shot. Indeed, in real life, the wing commander was busted for negligence.'

However, what would be the procedure followed by the MOD once the documents had been returned? Obviously Forsyth had to find out, as he told me: 'I did some research and was told that there was a brigadier (Capstick in the novel) who looked after the security inside the MOD. And that whole thing about procedure interested me. I asked: what if an anonymous package arrived at the MOD, what would be the procedure followed? Would the brigadier go to MI5 or MI6 and say I think we have a leak? I didn't know, so I did some more research.' Forsyth went back to the 'what would happen if . . . ?' factor.

> 'A false-flag?' mused Sir Patrick Strickland, from the Foreign Office. 'You mean he thought he was passing secrets to South Africa?'
>
> *The Fourth Protocol*

Forsyth looked into the intricacies of false-flag recruitment, as he explained: 'The man who held the documents (Berenson) in his safe was an extreme right winger who believed that he was working for South Africa. In fact, he was working for a South African who in turn was working for the Soviet Union.'

False-flag recruitment is an incredibly subtle intelligence gambit and can work brilliantly. Mosad, the Israeli intelligence agency, are past masters of it. The victim of false-flag recruitment believes that he/she is leaking information to a country/agency

The young master at work. To this day Forsyth favours the typewriter over the computer.

Above: The original UK film poster for *The Day of the Jackal* (1973) Forsyth's favourite film based upon one of his novels. Ronald Grant Archive

Right: Edward Fox as the Jackel, taking careful aim. Ronald Grant Archive

Above: Forsyth signs for his fans. *The Odessa File* book signing,1972.

Below: Jon Voigt as journalist Peter Miller in an action scene from one of his very best movies, *The Odessa File*, 1974.

Forsyth (right) on the set of *The Fourth Protocol* (1987) with Prince Michael of Kent (centre).

Stylish and imposing. Forsyth in the mid-80s.

Above: Still happy to sign. Frederick Forsyth signs *The Veteran*, September 2001.
Brian Aldrich

Left: Craig Cabell and Frederick Forsyth at the Langham Hilton, September 2001.
Brian Aldrich

The plot thickens.

that he/she has sympathies with while, in reality, that is just a screen. So in *The Fourth Protocol*, a British traitor believes he is leaking documentation to South Africa, when in truth, he is leaking secrets to the Soviet Union. The Soviets then conceived a cunning plan.

> 'I'm afraid we seem to have come across a small problem,'
> said Sir Nigel when he was seated. 'One of our civil servants
> in the Defence Ministry turns out to have been a bad egg.'
> 'Oh for Christ's sake, Nigel, not another leak,'
> expostulated Fox.
>
> *The Fourth Protocol*

The Fourth Protocol took in many different ideas and really gave the real-life British intelligence agencies something to think about, as Forsyth explained: 'After the book, remedial measures were taken, as much as they can be taken, to stop the idea of somebody coming into the country with a nuclear suitcase.'

Again, Forsyth had written a ground-breaking novel, but could he keep up the pace with his next?

12

The Negotiator

To the men of the Special Forces of the free world.

dedication to The Negotiator

FORSYTH'S SIXTH novel – his ninth book including non-fiction and short fiction – was *The Negotiator* (1989).

The Negotiator is a book largely ignored by Forsyth's critics and fans nowadays, which is unfortunate, because it included his most shocking and memorable opening chapter – the Prologue itself. Barely over a page long, it details a kidnap negotiation that goes badly wrong: a ten-year-old child is killed.

It is rare for Forsyth to hurt a child in his novels, for they are the innocent who must be protected at all costs; they don't understand or play the adult games Forsyth's fiction concentrates upon. Forsyth is not alone in this philosophy, as (another bestselling writer) horror novelist James Herbert adopts the same moral code. Although Herbert killed a baby in his first novel – *The Rats* (1974) – he has been reluctant to do so since; mainly because it was unnecessary. However, in the case of *The Negotiator*, the death of a child was important to Forsyth's plot, as it formed an appreciation of a central character (Quinn), not forgetting a hell of a shockwave to start a novel and grip the reader:

He could see the fright in her huge eyes, the little white teeth in her screaming mouth... and then bright crimson rose that bloomed on the front of her thin cotton dress. She went down then as if punched in the back...

The Negotiator

Having killed off the child in the Prologue, Forsyth then began to slowly unfold his story. He had clearly given the reader enough action to begin with and, because there was much for the reader to understand before the beef of the story – political intrigue – he spent approximately 80 pages detailing meetings and various documentation between characters.

In the wake of the dying American Secret Serviceman's radio call many things began to happen exceedingly fast. The snatch of the President's only son had taken place at 7.05 a.m. The radio call was logged at 7.07. The call was heard in three places.

The Negotiator

Although well thought-out and well executed, *The Negotiator* is little more than a straightforward thriller. No worldwide calamities, just a rattling good yarn that sold in droves. However, more was expected from Forsyth on this occasion, mainly because *The Negotiator* was the book that followed *The Fourth Protocol* and although both novels build up their intricate plots in a similar way – through political theories emanating from a Communist source – *The Negotiator* lacks the guts of a story that *The Fourth Protocol* had in abundance; even the thrill of the chase is played down somewhat.

The storyline to *The Negotiator* ran thus: an Oxford University student, who just happens to be the son of the President of the United States, is kidnapped. The biggest operation the British police have ever staged follows. President John Cormack is about to sign a disarmament treaty with the Soviets, but there are men close to him who believe that America can only survive a pending oil shortage by obtaining control of one of the richest Middle Eastern states. Cormack would never sanction such a move but what if he is forced to? And what if a traitor is watching the President's demise and reporting it to the Kremlin?

> The Director of the Secret Service, Creighton Burbank, had from the outset protested that the President's son should not be studying at all during the incumbency.
>
> *The Negotiator*

So the President's son has been kidnapped to immobilise the signing of the radical disarmament treaty with the Soviets. And it is here that things really begin to hot up and Forsyth begins to unfold the plot further.

Enter *The Negotiator*: Quinn. A man who 'never seems to use his first name':

> 'The man's a rebel,' said Donaldson with distaste, as he closed the file. 'He's a loner, a maverick, and a violent one at that. I think we may have made a mistake here.'
>
> *The Negotiator*

Quinn is unorthodox. Although a veteran of the Special Forces, he hates violence. Nothing new in that. People who see and take part in too much violence always end up opposed to it.

So Quinn is now *The Negotiator*. A man hounded by past killings and past treachery, who must strive for a peaceful solution despite his more natural violent instincts.

Quinn is unlike Sam McCready – The Deceiver – who appeared in Forsyth's next novel, but there is nothing of the

'George Smiley' look about him (unlike McCready). Females don't mother Quinn, he's a little too cool. Indeed, there's something James Bond-like about him:

'Is there anything else I can offer you, sir, anything at all?' drawled a honeyed voice in his ear.
He turned and grinned with relief. Sam stood in the aisle, leaning over him.
'Just you baby.'

The Negotiator

Like the killing of a child, Forsyth doesn't really engage in too many love scenes in his fiction. However, he admits to a 'bit of an affair' in *The Devil's Alternative* as he does in *The Negotiator*. So, essentially, *The Negotiator* was quite a departure in style for Forsyth, what with a child being killed off and an uncustomary love interest it is possible that Forsyth dreamed up the idea of *The Negotiator* after Margaret Thatcher's son – Mark Thatcher – had gone missing on the Dakar Rally in the Algerian desert, an incident which Forsyth actually mentioned in the book, going on to speculate about the Prime Minister's hurt:

Then, in the privacy of the night she cried from that pure and very special pain felt by a parent whose child is in danger. Mark Thatcher had been found alive by a patrol after six days.

The Negotiator

So all Forsyth had to do was substitute the British Prime Minister for the American President and swap the misadventures of the son for a kidnap for political gain?
Perhaps I do him a slight injustice here. As usual, *The Negotiator* was meticulously researched. Forsyth personally

visited every place depicted in the story with the exception of Vietnam. He had already been to the USA countless times, however, for *The Negotiator*, he returned with a list of contacts in government and the covert world, as he explained to me in September 2000: 'There were extensive interviews with the CIA, the FBI, the White House staff, and experts in hostage negotiations. For the rest, I just wandered about and asked the usual daft questions.'

Although *The Negotiator* was a hugely successful novel, it doesn't pack the punch of some of Forsyth's other books. The scale of the worldwide catastrophe is somewhat played down, and the characters find themselves a little stifled.

13

'...a sort of unleashed Ghenkhis Khan'

Thrillers nowadays have to be accurate. Can't get away with vague generalizations. Look at Le Carré, Clancey – you think they don't research every last detail? It's the only way nowadays.

The Deceiver

SAM McCREADY is the Deceiver. A Secret Intelligence Officer in the Secret Intelligence Service (SIS) whose job it is to feed disinformation to the Communists, but with the Cold War at an end – and only a few years to go before early retirement – McCready finds that his superiors – who seem about 'as controllable as Ghenkhis Khan' – wish to close his department. However, as they are fond of 'Sam', they offer him three alternative posts – all non-jobs – in order to encourage him to stay in the Service he has so diligently served over the years.

There is only one thing for McCready to do: appeal against the closure of his department – Deception, Disinformation and Psychological Operations (Dee-Dee and Psy Ops). A special hearing is held, chaired by Deputy Chief of SIS, Timothy Edwards.

You do not become, however recently, Chief of the Secret

Intelligence Service – the SIS – without developing a certain wariness when confronted by such warmth from a relative stranger. Sir Mark steeled himself for a difficult meeting.

The Deceiver

The bosses represent the system – the 'old school tie' brigade – an antiquated, self-indulgent system that still creaked on through the years like an OAP's much-relied-upon walking cane. But the system still worked. It was the 'tried and proved' method that every civil servant must appreciate or pay the consequences.

The Deceiver clearly showed what Forsyth thought of the traditional government department: the frustrations, the in-fighting, lack of loyalty – not just traitors – but by the department on those who had served it so well over the years.

The Deceiver was a book based on the paranoia of the Cold War, or perhaps more accurately, the only paranoia left after the Cold War: that which is in your own department.

When the Berlin Wall came down and the Cold War thawed, it wasn't just SIS officers who were looking over their shoulder for the golden handshake, it was the thriller writers too. What would the likes of Craig Thomas (*Firefox*), John Le Carré (*The Spy Who Came in From the Cold*) and Frederick Forsyth do?

Suddenly, some of their fiction exuded a quaintness because with the Cold War over, the mistrust in the Soviet Union was suddenly misplaced.

However, with *The Deceiver*, Forsyth could get away with writing about the Cold War, because – as a novel – it was really the final conclusion to that paranoia.

People betray their countries for many reasons. With Russians, it was usually a deep disillusionment with the lies and corruption they saw all around them.

The Deceiver

Obviously some people will always turn their back on their country, join the 'other side'; but instead of anger and intrigue, there is a feeling of nostalgia about *The Deceiver*. We know it's the end of an era, which is probably why we take extra enjoyment from a passage like: 'Both men had reason to prefer the gloom, for one was a traitor and the other a spy.' We suddenly become nostalgia freaks, but then again, how many Cold War novels have we enjoyed since *The Deceiver*? Clearly, the book was the right thing released at the right time.

In 1992, novelist Craig Thomas explained to me how the end of the Cold War affected his own brand of thriller: 'The techno thriller has had its day, because it was the Cold War that made us frightened of machines.' But what would Thomas do next? He explained, 'Modern adventure. Where writers use their own travels to create a story.' Indeed, this was something Forsyth did to great success in *The Deceiver*, and in September 2000 told me that he agreed with Craig Thomas's above-mentioned comments: 'I think Craig is probably right. The modern adventure is the way forward. The Cold War has been over for ten years, so that contest between the West and the USSR is over.'

So has the backdrop of Cold War fiction gone for ever? Forsyth thinks not. 'To resuscitate the Cold War story today would not be a very good idea. Maybe in 15 years' time there may be some market as there is with Vietnam today, because Vietnam stories were not popular in the States for 15 years after the war happened.'

So where do we go now? Who is the enemy? Forsyth explained: 'Well, directly after *The Deceiver*, as now: Saddam Hussein.'

To complete the loop, novelist Campbell Armstrong (*Jig*, *Agents of Darkness*) told me in 1994, 'There are so many opportunities to do new things. I look at the holes in Europe...and I see so many more story plot-lines there.'

Thriller writers don't have to dwell in the past, as there's so much going on in the world today, as Forsyth explained in *The Deceiver*: 'There's a bloody dangerous world out there, and it's not getting less dangerous, but more so.'

So the tide turned and the thriller genre dropped its cold exterior, as Forsyth confirmed in his dedication for *The Deceiver*: 'The Cold War lasted forty years. For the record, the West won it. But not without cost. This book is for those who spent so much of their lives in the shadowed places. Those were the days, my friends.'

Perhaps the premature retirement of Sam McCready (in the book) symbolised the changes Forsyth knew he had to make in order to continue his career as a globe-trotting novelist. At a Royal United Services Institute (RUSI) lecture in March 2001, during a question and answer session, Forsyth told the floor, 'I spoke to my "spooky" friends [top civil servants he had befriended over the years], and they told me that despite the end of the Cold War, three things would remain unchanged. They were: one – espionage: two – retention of nuclear deterrent: three – continued use of Special Forces.' So Forsyth still had a clear way forward with his thriller writing. But before we analyse this change – which really came about with his next novel *The Fist of God* – let us look at *The Deceiver* a little more closely.

Sam McCready has to fight for his job. To do this, he has to justify it through different case studies, clearly showing the many skills he has employed in his work and, ostensibly, his continued validity to the department.

So, after setting the scene with a brief introduction, Forsyth presents the reader with four novellas, each a separate adventure in the life of Sam McCready – the Deceiver.

In three years they would pension him off. There would be a

small party in the office, Aust would make a speech, and he would be gone. To what?

The Deceiver

McCready knows that he is just another expendable cog in an ever-changing system – good man or not. There will always be good men – and women – as the government Service is a self-healing body, the new cells always replace the old. McCready knows that the end of the Cold War doesn't mean a more optimistic future; there will always be threats, some worse than those posed by the Soviet Union and, yes, he wants to be part of that battle, for God's sake he enjoys his job:

> The gathering of intelligence is a strange business. Rarely does one single coup provide all the answers, let alone solve all the problems. Mostly, the picture appears piece by piece, as in a jigsaw.

The Deceiver

The Deceiver started life as a series of six screenplay treatments that Forsyth wrote for LWT (see Film Guide in Part Three). He then chose four of them for his 'novelisation'. Essentially, *The Deceiver is* a novel, as it unfolds the story of one man's career through individual case studies. Each story is linked together to show the effect of each upon Sam McCready's Hearing, until inevitably, we reach the final conclusion.

By the time he started writing *The Deceiver*, Forsyth was divorced from his first wife and was now living with his future second wife, Sandy. However, despite this dramatic turnaround in his personal life – a new lease-of-love – two of the first women we meet in *The Deceiver* are far from endearing: a high-class prostitute and Bruno Morenz's (a main character in the story 'Pride and Extreme Prejudice') wife Irmtraut 'a woman of quite bovine stupidity and potato-like contours...'

The first operation reviewed in Sam McCready's Hearing ('Pride and Extreme Prejudice') concerns a mission to trace a German-born agent who has had a complete nervous breakdown. Bruno Morenz has a loveless marriage, so he has an affair with a prostitute. Morenz believes that she is deeply in love with him but then discovers that that is far from the truth. When he enters her flat unannounced, he finds her in bed with a younger man laughing at a video of the middle-aged Morenz attempting to make love to her. His world suddenly collapses. He loses his head and shoots the couple and goes into hiding. From here on in, a Cold War story is woven together.

This case doesn't help Sam McCready's appeal. Although McCready performed well during that particular operation, Timothy Edwards is keen to state: '"Thank you for reminding us of the events in 1985 ... though I feel one might point out that in intelligence terms that year now constitutes a different and even vanished age."'

The next operation reviewed (entitled 'The Price of the Bride') concerned a KGB colonel – Orlov – who quietly slips away from an exercise on Salisbury Plain (in the south of England) but gives himself up to the CIA instead of the British government. The story then goes on to illustrate the friction between British and US intelligence services but, perhaps more interestingly, how they must overcome their differences in order to ascertain if Colonel Orlov is genuine, i.e. is he a true defector?

Obviously, McCready comes up with the answer, but Edwards, although impressed with his subordinate's work during that operation, is unsure if those talents would be called for again.

It is now becoming clear that McCready has some enemies within the hallowed corridors of Whitehall and the end of the Cold War has only strengthened the position of those 'career mandarins', but the Hearing continues its bloody course with the details of a third operation (entitled 'A Casualty of War'). In April

1986, fighters from both the United States of America and Great Britain attacked the private living quarters of Colonel Gaddafi outside Tripoli. Gaddafi survived, although he suffered a nervous breakdown. He then vowed to take his revenge against the United States and Great Britain: ' "In the early spring of 1987 we learned how Gaddafi intended to extract that revenge upon Britain, and the case was given to Sam McCready... " '

Gaddafi planned to ship arms to the IRA – two years after they (the IRA) had had 'talks' with him – in order to mount his revenge on the West. As there was nothing like the IRA in the United States, Gaddafi wanted an American diplomat killed in the attack on Britain.

Obviously, the IRA was only too happy to help – and take a useful supply of arms for their own consumption into the bargain – so McCready was assigned the case to thwart the plan.

Although the story has a satisfying conclusion, the outcome – as far as McCready's Hearing is concerned – was indifference. However, the final operation (entitled 'A Little Bit of Sunshine') was entirely different. For this was when McCready really covered himself in glory, one of his biggest success stories in his career: his control of a Caribbean island after a political murder has taken place.

There is no doubt that on that occasion McCready does nothing less than putting in a relevant and exemplary performance, although in perhaps an unorthodox manner. It is probably this aspect that fails to persuade Timothy Edwards to keep McCready, but then again he had – no doubt – made up his mind already.

Westminster Bridge rose before him. Across it the Houses of Parliament, whose freedom and occasional foolishness he had spent thirty years trying to protect, towered against the blue sky.

The Deceiver

The feeling at the end of the book – for McCready – is dissatisfaction and possibly regret. For he has given the best part of his life to the loyal service of the Realm but found little reward. However, there is something more in the sub-text, Forsyth's own tearful farewell to a particular way of writing.

The Deceiver wasn't just the end of an era for Frederick Forsyth, it was the end of a whole genre. But where would he go next?

Four weeks later, Saddam Hussein invaded Kuwait.

The Deceiver

14

Qubeth-ut-Allah

We don't shy away from supporting moral dimensions in war. However, we have to be objective about who we support. We just can't send in troops because a group of people are likeable; the decision must be made for more sound reasons, i.e. we don't ban fox-hunting because there's a public outcry. We don't back down because of media pressure. When a decision is made, it is made because it is the right decision, not because we feel sorry for a particular group of people.

Frederick Forsyth speaking at RUSI, March 2001

AT 10 O'CLOCK Gulf time on the morning of 2 August 1990, Iraq invaded Kuwait. The Western world quickly rushed to the Kuwaitis' aid.

A major operation began to take shape, grandly titled 'Desert Shield'. Britain invested millions in their military action against Iraq. Government contracts officers worked overtime to purchase and send hardware out to the Gulf where the kit was put to immediate use.

Saddam Hussein promised 'the mother of all wars', which clearly didn't happen. After a half-hearted effort by Iraqi troops, the war was over and Hussein had lost (however, he would later claim some small victory after observing that come the millennium he was still the Iraqi ruler while the leaders of his Western enemies had long been dethroned).

Over this great 'theatrical production' that was the Gulf War, Forsyth cast a sceptical eye, as he told me in November 1999: 'My instinct was the journalistic instinct. There were unanswered questions, but that's how my thrillers come about. I've never really stopped being a journalist – not a muck-raker – but an investigator and I'm convinced that the Establishment only really tells us ten per cent – if that – of what actually goes on and only a small proportion of the rest of the media find out.'

There was obviously the basis of a good thriller here but Forsyth had to work out what it was. His initial feeling of disquiet was prompted by watching an item about the war on the evening news, as he told me, 'At the end of the Gulf War I thought, 'This is simply too damn pat. We've watched this on television for weeks and it's run like a production. I wanted the credits to role at the end of it, I wanted to see who wrote the script. I also wanted to know who the producer and the director were.

'Nothing can be that perfect, because everyone knows that in a war everything is incredibly messy. Ten per cent of all plans go pear-shaped and here we were reeling with such incredible efficiency from the Allied Forces.'

So Forsyth began to investigate, as he told me: 'I found that we missed most of the targets, even with all the smart bombs and laser-guided weapons.

'We didn't know about half of what we should have targeted, because all the targets were under the desert – laboratories manufacturing germ warfare and there was also an attempt at nuclear warfare. Now we didn't hear about any of that. That was discovered when the United Nations team went in after the war and said, "Oh my God, we didn't hit a third of what was dangerous here."

'We weren't told that the SAS were in the Iraqi desert for most of the war. I think I said it first and then *Bravo Two Zero* came out. But again, not even the SAS got it right, even some of their plans went pear-shaped.'

> On 11 April British Customs officers seized on the docks of Middlesbrough eight sections of huge steel pipes, beautifully forged and milled and able to be assembled by giant flanges at each end, drilled to take powerful nuts and bolts. Triumphant officers announced that these tubes were not for a petrochemical plant as specified on the bills of lading and the export certificates but were parts of a great gun barrel ... destined for Iraq.
>
> *The Fist of God*

Forsyth took his facts about the Gulf War and connected them with something else. 'Nobody mentioned the big gun that was discovered in the spring of 1990 – in a flurry of media coverage – what was called the Super Gun. Indeed, after the initial media show nobody mentioned it again. But where did it go? Did we intercept all the major components that made it? I found that interesting, because I thought if that ever fired a nuclear shell it could fly a thousand kilometres. It didn't fire. But there were more questions about the war, such as, why did Saddam fire scuds at Israel?

'There was so much to reveal, so much to expose.'

Forsyth spent a year researching *The Fist of God* and it would eventually become his personal favourite amongst his many novels.

The Fist of God was a topical action adventure, thought-provoking and detailed, full of larger-than-life characters both

fictional and real. But what was more important was Forsyth's
capacity to show that he could write about something other than
corruption from either a Communist – or Capitalist – source. He
was finding the new direction he needed.

Forsyth has always laboured over the opening line of a book. He
admits to being 'quite pleased' with the opening of *The Fist of
God*: 'The man with ten minutes to live was laughing.' Instantly it
grabs the reader, but unlike lesser thrillers, the tension and excitement doesn't dissipate over the next 494 pages – it increases.

The Fist of God was Frederick Forsyth back on a roll – with
nothing to do with the Cold War – so in a way, it outshone *The
Devil's Alternative* and *The Fourth Protocol* in as much as this
was an up-to-date thriller that didn't fulfil the criteria of a tried-
and-proved genre against an old foe. The story: on the eve of the
Gulf War British Intelligence learns that Saddam Hussein has a
deadly weapon he calls Qubeth-ut-Allah – the Fist of God. An
SAS man – Major Mike Martin – is sent into the desert disguised
as a Bedouin – Mahoud Al-Khouri. He is selected for the job
because of his unique position: his skin colour and his pedigree
mean he can pass himself off as an Arab.

Martin goes into occupied Kuwait, recruiting along the way a
small band of rebels who cause a few minor distractions. From
this the Bedouin gains a reputation with the enemy and they
begin to track him down. Martin must find a spy code-named
Jericho. He is informed that this man will trade military secrets –
at a price. He then goes off to the bazaars to find his man.

Paxman's second fear was that Martin had been caught,
tortured and 'turned', that he was now broadcasting under
duress. He rejected the idea as unlikely.

The Fist of God

Martin's assignment takes him through the whole length of the

Gulf War in heroic style. There is nothing of the good clean-cut hero about Martin, he is a deep, gritty, sand-blasted individual whose duty to Queen and Country is clear.

Couldn't possibly offer you a decent sole *meunière* at Scott's, could I? You know it, of course. Mount Street.

The Fist of God

But for all this gung-ho boys-own adventure, Forsyth doesn't lose sight of the plot. As usual he lets the story unfold slowly. And then we find a traditional thriller theme, the clandestine meeting at a restaurant (in fact this is how Major Martin is selected to go into Kuwait). Steven Laing is a member of the Secret Intelligence Service (SIS) and needs to recruit a man to go into the desert. He has lunch with colleague Terry Martin and after too much 'Meursault and port with his lunch', Martin tells Laing that the best man for the job in Kuwait would be his brother Major Mike Martin of the SAS.

This tasteful little vignette shows the subtlety of Forsyth's style. He knows when to hang back, to include procedure and detail, clearly showing the souce of all the intricate strands of his story. But there's something else here too. Including a restaurant scene like this says a lot about Forsyth himself. He's a traditionalist. The right man to talk politics with politicians and farming with farmers, over lunch of course. Indeed, above Forsyth's favourite table in the dining room of London's Montcalm Hotel there is a plaque that states that Frederick Forsyth has interviewed spies and assassins there; or as Forsyth would state: 'Mercenaries, psychopaths, international arms dealers and ex-Nazis.'

However, there is one other aspect to appreciate with this restaurant scene: Forsyth enjoys good food and good wine – especially good Claret: 'ruby in colour... and normally grown on the slopes of Bordeaux' (as he observed in his short story 'The

Art of the Matter', 2001). This, essentially, is nothing new; other established writers in the past have clearly shown their passion for good restaurants and cuisine, such as Graham Greene and Dennis Wheatley (*The Human Factor* and *Gateway to Hell*), so in that respect, Forsyth keeps a true-blue British tradition going with a spot of well-timed lunch.

> The Iron Lady soon got the impression that her good friend was about to start wavering again. Within two hours she put a broom handle so far up the President's left trouser leg that it came out near the collar line.
>
> *The Fist of God*

With the books *The Negotiator*, *The Fist of God* and *Icon*, Forsyth included a cast list – a dramatis personae – which included both real-life and fictional characters that would appear throughout the book. Obviously, Forsyth had used real-life figures in his very first novel, such as Charles de Gaulle or even Simon Weisenthal in *The Odessa File*, but with the novels he released between 1989 and 1996 – with the exception of *The Deceiver* – he included politicians who were still in power, obviously Margaret Thatcher, but also a host of others. In October 2000, Michael Heseltine told me how he felt about being placed in a Frederick Forsyth novel: 'I think Forsyth's books are wonderful. He doesn't write about people in a libellous way. It never affects a person politically, so I have no problem with it.'

In a way, it is a frowned-upon gambit to use real-life people in fiction, mainly because of the potential problem of libel action, but Forsyth has it down to a fine art. But by including real-life characters, he increases the amount of intrigue going on in a reader's mind. What with the public demand for 'more truth', especially when dealing with government departments (dare we misquote 'the truth is in there'), Forsyth's fiction takes on an extra validity in the current marketplace.

The Fist of God was a prime example of the best of the Forsyth style: his natural gift of storytelling, his journalistic eye for research (good government contacts). But was all this getting a little too easy for him?

During the promotion for the paperback of *The Fist of God* in 1995, Forsyth hinted that it could be. 'I might decide that the day has come for the last of the covert thrillers and try something else. But fiction is more fun than non-fiction.' For the time being he was content to write the conventional thrillers. But would he still feel content to write them after his next novel?

The long black Mercedes eased under the arch and out into Staraya Ploshchad. In the back of the limousine Josef Cherkassov, the President of Russia, sat alone, slumped in thought.

Icon

15

Icon

By the summer of 1999 the days of five-thousand roubles to the dollar of mid-nineties were memory. The wheat crop...had failed twice, in '97 and '98, and the crop from Siberia was delayed until it rotted because the partisans blew away the rail tracks. In the cities bread prices spiralled. President Cherkassov clung to office but was clearly no longer in power.

Icon

ALTHOUGH WE can look back upon *Icon* (not unlike *Nineteen Eighty-Four* and *2001: A Space Odyssey*) and say 'that never happened', the book – like its sci-fi counterparts – had elements of truth; also some tantalising questions, such as: could another Adolf Hitler come to power and push a down-trodden state back on its feet again? And perhaps more importantly: could such a madman become the president of a so-called Super Power?

As usual, Forsyth researched *Icon* thoroughly. He spoke to KGB defectors, British Intelligence and ex-CIA men, he also went to Russia – the book's main setting – and came to the conclusion that his idea was no leap of faith, indeed a psychotic dictator *could* become president of such a nation, as he explained to me in March 2000, 'To begin with I started with the idea, could it be possible for the ultra-right type of dictator to arrive and take the presidency of Russia and turn it into – essentially – a fascist state?

An interesting concept, but where did Forsyth get his original idea? He explained, 'We always assume that Russia must be Communist; what I became intrigued by – from the early 90s onwards – was the rise of racism which came out of nowhere in Russia at an extraordinary speed. So, yes, another Adolf Hitler could emerge. But then we had the question: what could the West do to stop him? The answer was probably nothing, except raise some privateers.'

Marchbanks nodded. 'There seems to be nothing to stop Igor Komarov from taking the Presidency.'

Icon

There are always uncertainties at election time. For a short space of time chaos reigns, the politicians (and next door neighbours – who wears red, who wears blue?) are at each other's throats. In every sense of the cliché people show their true colours. Or do they?

Well, possibly the people may, but what about the politicians themselves? 'Politics is very much like a conjuring trick. You know something sneaky is going on but you can't quite put your finger on it,' observes Lord Janner, and he's probably right.

There is generally nothing life-threatening to fear from another change of government. But what if a politician's motives are a little bit more 'sneaky', and he is about to be elected premier?

Suddenly we have the backbone to a Frederick Forsyth thriller and in the case of *Icon*, his last for more than five years.

It is quite easy to underplay *Icon*, not because the story itself is quite basic but solely because it is set in 1999 – when we know there was no election crisis in Russia. So on this occasion we can say that the novel is provably incorrect. However, the novel's strengths are the devious intricacies of the extreme leader's (Ivor Komarov's) rise to power and the subtleties of political eco-systems, in Russia and the West.

The basic story is: Komarov's trusty assistant has failed to lock away a secret document that is essentially the details of Komarov's Black Manifesto. It is stolen by a cleaner, an old man known as 'the Rabbit'. The document then finds its way into Western hands who are keen to find out if the document is genuine. If it is, they must work out what to do about it?

Jason Monk is the man selected to answer the questions and lead the operation. The Black Manifesto must be countered, but Monk – the ex-CIA man – has got an uphill struggle. 'By 1999 the total employment figure for security men across the Russian nation was 800,000 and a third of them were in Moscow.'

Komarov promises the oppressed people of Russia a change for the better and they believe him. He is high in the opinion poll; but what will be the consequences of his election victory?

The thought process begins.

Icon is one of Forsyth's most politically stimulating novels, sharing some comparisons with *The Devil's Alternative* – Russia on the brink of famine and consequently political disaster – which was his first true political thriller and, along with *The Fourth Protocol* and *The Fist of God*, one of his most important books. But, as hinted at during the promotion round to *The Fist of God*, Forsyth was now becoming unsettled. In 1996 – shortly after the release of *Icon* – the media announced that Forsyth had retired. That, however, wasn't true, as he told me in August 2000, 'Everyone wanted a headline. After *Icon* I said that I didn't want to write any more thrillers. But a much better headline was "Forsyth doesn't want to write any more novels". I never said "never". I said that I had reached the end of the road for thrillers, but I would like to write other types of book. I was asked "what types?" and I said that I didn't know, because at the time I didn't.'

But why didn't he want to write any more thrillers? He told me: 'Because it was too easy. I felt stuck in a rut.'

Too easy, yes, but still quite lucrative?

'Yes. But it depends on your personality,' he told me. 'Don't forget I had been writing the same type of book for 26 years. For me it got very samey. There wasn't a challenge there any more. I knew how to write a thriller and I had set up this expectant audience, so there was this presumption that I would go on doing the same thing.'

You didn't want to appear predictable?

'I just felt stuck in a rut. I don't mind writing the occasional thriller but I wanted to branch out and see if I could do something else.

'*The Shepherd* was very popular in its little way... It wasn't about violence, it wasn't about spies, it was a ghost story for God's sake. It almost had spiritual undertones. And it was popular.

'Shortly after *The Shepherd* I wrote an anthology called *No Comebacks*, one of the stories was about violence – the first one – but the other nine stories in the book didn't have anything to do with violence at all although they all had a sting in the tail.'

No Comebacks – like *The Shepherd* – proved to be a very popular book too, so in a way Forsyth felt he was selling himself short. He knew he was capable of writing other types of accessible fiction and he should attempt to do so again, as he told me, 'I've actually proved that I could write other types of fiction, wear a number of different hats and that's what I decided to do.'

It took Forsyth three years to come up with something different. By the time *The Phantom of Manhattan* was released,

Forsyth had picked up a CBE and had sold 60 million copies of his books in over thirty languages.

Pushing on the power he turned the Foxy Lady away from the island and out towards the lonely sea and the sky.

Icon

16

Not the Usual Fare

The Man was masked as ever but I knew when I saw him that it was he who had been the Union Officer who had sung that amazing duet with the prima donna at the opera house and brought the audience to tears.

The Phantom of Manhattan

THE CONCLUSION to Forsyth's 30th year as a novelist was not dissimilar to the finale of one of his thrillers. It would have its very own sting in the tail: his first gothic novel.

To write a sequel to a classic novel has always been an unpopular gambit, however Forsyth decided to write the sequel to Gaston Leroux's *The Phantom of the Opera* only after contacting Andrew Lloyd Webber. This is an important point, as Forsyth's *The Phantom of Manhattan* – his tenth novel – was a sequel to Andrew Lloyd Webber's musical production of *The Phantom of the Opera*, rather than Leroux's original novel. An interesting gambit in itself. But not surprising, as Forsyth proved – in his preface to the book – that Leroux's original research was not reliable, so it is not difficult to appreciate why he favoured the musical version rather than the original novel; as he qualified to me in March 2000, 'Leroux tried to create a faction novel –

part fact, part fiction – but if you're going to do that, those things you claim are checkable must be checked, and those things you claim are not checkable must be unconfirmed either way, such as: 1 September 1939, Hitler invaded Poland, the same morning a man with perfectly forged papers arrived at Berlin railway station and stepped into a waking city.

'The first point is a fact; the second you can neither confirm nor deny. Shoving them together sometimes gives the impression that they both should be true, because we know the first one is, we assume the other one is too.

'But Leroux didn't do that. He made claims that were quite provably untrue. As I read his book, I noticed it wasn't in chronological order. He jumped all over the place. He also couldn't work out in his mind what the Phantom was. Was he a damaged man, so a more sinned against than sinning man, or was he a deranged sadist. He flitted from one to the other. So one moment you're thinking, Oh, poor Erik, and the next you're recoiling in horror.

'It wasn't – I thought – a very well-thought-out book. But it did create a legend, so somewhere in amongst the dross was this nugget of a very appealing story. What Andrew Lloyd Webber did in his musical was cut out all the nonsense and stick to the basic story. Where he differed from all the previous films was he said, "This isn't a monster story, it's a beauty and the beast story." He's a physical beast but not a moral beast. So, as I put it to my editor, Leroux gave him a face, Andrew gave him a heart, now I thought I'd give him a soul as well.'

With the way Erik moves from France to Manhattan (in Forsyth's sequel), the scenes of ridicule and squalor at the fun fair – let alone wearing a mask – conjure comparisons between Forsyth's Phantom and the characterisation of John Merrick, the elephant man. I asked Forsyth about this imagery and if he thought of John Merrick at all; he told me, 'The elephant man obviously wasn't a novel. It was an actual clinical case, and he wasn't deformed from birth. He had a growth that grew and grew and grew, until it finally consumed his whole face. Obviously, an attempt was made to rectify the deformity, and he became a celebrity because of that. So he wore a mask.

'No, I didn't think of the elephant man. *The Phantom of the Opera* is a legend created by Leroux in 1911, following a visit to an opera in 1910, where he said he heard a rumour that up to 30 years earlier, there had been someone – a Phantom – dwelling deep in the bowels of the opera house. And on that he based his book.'

Leroux's original novel was popular for about three months before it died. It was resuscitated by Universal Pictures with the first Lon Chaney movie. There were three subsequent movies, a TV movie, a rock opera and then Andrew Lloyd Webber's version.

'*The Phantom* has become a bit of a legend, because it is now the most popular musical ever,' Forsyth told me. 'An estimated 60 million people have seen it. I saw the show years ago, then I read the book, saw the show again, then conferred with Andrew about it.'

One can picture the peer and the novelist sitting down to an after-dinner conversation and conceiving the idea of a sequel to Webber's musical, as Andrew Lloyd Webber confirmed in March 2001: 'Wherever it may have been, and I suspect it was probably over an excess of rather too much good claret, somehow we both got hooked on how the Phantom story could be continued. Freddie, by the way, like myself, share's Erik's love of the finest French vinicular products. Gaston Leroux tells us that the Phantom had one of the best cellars in Paris.'

What intrigued Forsyth about Andrew Lloyd Webber's musical was the continuation of the Phantom legend; as he told me in March 2000, 'We know Quasimodo died, that King Arthur died, that Robin Hood died. We do not know at the end of Andrew's musical what the hell happens to the Phantom. All we know is he walks away into the shadows. Clearly he is not dying, he's not old. There are unanswered questions. So *The Phantom of Manhattan* is my version of what happened next.'

There was a concern that Andrew Lloyd Webber didn't like Forsyth's version, a rumour Forsyth was keen to expel: 'Andrew has told me repeatedly that he does like it. But he, too, had been somewhat exercised by the unanswered questions and he was happy to accept my way of answering them. Obviously, with a murder charge hanging over Erik's head, he had to flee France, indeed Europe. And at that time – the end of the 19th century – America would have been an obvious answer, because millions of Europeans were fleeing West to a new life. So into this world the Phantom would go. It was logical.'

Obviously a lot of research went into *The Phantom of Manhattan*, but despite the criticism of Leroux and his original Paris-based novel, Forsyth did very little research in France, as he explained: 'I didn't do much research there. I did check out the kind of hospice Madame Giry would die in, and I also checked another hospital that I used in the book. But the rest of my research was done in New York. I went there to research the city at the turn of the 20th century. Physically, there's none of it left, but there are records and photographs. I found horrible poverty amongst immigrant ghettos, but a few hundred yards away, staggering wealth. It was a most extraordinary city, because it was incredibly vibrant. It was a city where you could arrive penniless and become a millionaire within a few years. You couldn't do that anywhere else but New York, if of course, you had the talent.'

We journalists are never destined to be loved. Like cops, this is something we just have to accept if we want to take up our strange career.

The Phantom of Manhattan

But for all this, *The Phantom of Manhattan* was an unorthodox move for Forsyth. It was a very emotional novel, dealing with relationships – love and lust – a style more favoured by female readers than his traditional male readership. He explained the motive for his actions: 'I like to think that I can wear a number of hats. I'm known for the thriller hat. I think I was a reasonably good journalist – years ago – before I turned to novels, that I have a reasonably analytical mind, with a capacity to research. I'm not afraid of hard work and I'm also reasonably imaginative. I just thought that after 30 years of writing thrillers I was in a little bit of a rut. So I thought I'd do something else, if the public would accept me.'

He said in that noiseless clearing he could hear silent screams... But over all this, he said, he could hear something else. There was in that clearing a lost soul, crying in agony like Coleridge's wandering albatross...

The Phantom of Manhattan

The ending of Forsyth's book is very operatic. This was partially steered by Andrew Lloyd Webber, who said, 'For my part, one of the principal concerns was that the story should end in both tragedy and optimism.' Indeed it does, clearly showing a side to Forsyth's writing rarely seen before: the writer of emotional fiction.

However, *The Phantom of Manhattan* was a clear change of genre and style for Forsyth, there was still evidence of his traditional trade marks: the thorough research – to the extent of writing a Preface showing where Leroux went wrong – and that endearing style of writing which exposes some of his greatest characters' passion for material wealth.

... the long passage floored and walled in solid gold. Oh, the

pleasure of gold. To touch, to caress, to feel, to own.
                                        The Phantom of Manhattan

Indeed, a quote like this could quite easily have come from Sir James Mason's mouth in *The Dogs of War*, so there was still something of the old Frederick Forsyth in *The Phantom of Manhattan*.

Although it is very easy to criticise the book because of its lower worldwide sales figures and departure in genre, praise must indeed go to Forsyth for his bravery in writing such a work. The passage of time will tell if *The Phantom of Manhattan* becomes a classic or not (bearing in mind that Gaston Leroux's novel was popular for approximately three months before disappearing).

The answer is quite possibly no. However, for people interested in Forsyth's work it will always be an intriguing departure, showcasing a more romantic side to the thriller writer – something rarely seen since the secret assignations in *The Devil's Alternative*, exactly 20 years before.

17

Dinner in the West End

AFTER THE release of *The Phantom of Manhattan*, Forsyth toyed with the idea of writing a book of short stories, as he told me in March 2000: 'I haven't really decided what I'm going to do next. Maybe a book of short stories. I did one once before. But I'm really not sure at the moment.'

So after *The Phantom of Manhattan* Forsyth was still keen to do something slightly different. He told me that he had considered doing 'something mildly autobiographical', but was unsure as to what. However, by September 2000 he had signed a contract with Internet company Online Originals for a set of five short stories he would jointly call *Quintet*.

Forsyth, by his own admission, is no slave to the Internet. In fact, he doesn't use it at all. His decision to write an E book really came from the sales pitch sold to him by Online Originals. Not that they tried to mislead him in any way. They didn't, but their enthusiasm was not backed by a horde of online shoppers, as Forsyth told me in February 2001: 'I was advised that more and more people were switching from normal product purchasing to E retailing. They were buying things on the Internet – or at least choosing them on the Internet – placing the order on the Internet, then paying for them by credit card whereupon they would suddenly arrive in the post by Jiffy bag.

'So this was a growing merchandising arm. And it was at this point – they said – occupying up to 30 per cent of retail merchandising and growing.

'That included bookshop purchasing like Amazon.com and the next stage of this – they said – (paying for your books on the net and having them come by Jiffy bag), was ordering them via the net and having them sent to you on the net.'

Forsyth was asked if he would like to be one of the pioneers of net shopping.

'Now I thought about this in a very detached way,' he told me. 'And I thought, I can't see people wanting to read 550 pages on a computer screen. I can't see them really wanting to download – that is, print out – 550 pages – on their home printer because it will be A4 in size and you would end up with something the size of a telephone directory.'

However, despite this logic, Forsyth was surprised to see another bestselling writer jump on the Internet bandwagon, as he told me, 'When Mr [Stephen] King said that he was going to do his next novel on the Internet, I raised my eyebrows. Then he said that he was going to do that book chapter by chapter. He called it *The Plant* – which sounded like it was a book about a runaway ivy, or a deranged bindweed – he said he was going to write one chapter a month, over ten months, and he was not going to encrypt them. He was going to put them out on his own website – monthly – and he would expect a dollar per chapter to be sent to him. And then he issued two provisos. One – because it was not encrypted, if people were just going to download it and not send him the money, he wouldn't go on. And two – if he didn't get 75 per cent – and he was trusting everybody – to pay the newsboy, he would cease with the story.

'I had two major queries with that. First, I couldn't see anyone waiting ten months for a climax, it's a hell of a long time to wait.

Because, if the book is a real page turner, people want to find out what happens at the end, and second, if the paying audience dips under 65 per cent by Chapter Five, and he says bugger you all, I'm not going on, what about the honest people who paid for the first five chapters? Would they have the basis for a class action, to say, "I want my money back"? I didn't know, so it struck me as a dodgy idea.

'On the other hand, I thought a short story has a beginning, a middle and an end. So I had in mind – specifically – short stories. Now there may well be a market to put them out as different market experiences, such as one select experience, one pay experience, one download experience. And having selected it, you have your short story. Then you can shove it in your attaché case and read it tomorrow on your flight to Athens!

'So on that basis I decided to go into the world of E books. Over the next 12 weeks, I began to write these stories. The perceived wisdom was that I would churn out one of these stories, Online Originals would edit it, encrypt it and transfer it to E information, then advertise the story on five separate webs.

'So I wrote the first one, the second one and then by the third one two things became plain. The first was that Stephen King was in deep trouble, having lost faith by Chapter Four of his book and stopped. The second thing was – and this was with my stories – I received call after call from people asking where they could find them.

'I explained where they were, but people were still having problems, spending up to two hours trying to download them.

'So I complained, told the company that no one could decrypt the stories, and they were quite genuinely surprised. But the problems still continued. My faith went completely down the swannee when one guy tried for four hours to download a story and still couldn't manage it. I had had enough by that time.

'I decided that the whole thing had been hyped out of its skull.

There is no way in my lifetime that E books are going to replace hardbacks and paperbacks.

'The other eye-opener was, after a while, I got my sales figures through and the first of my short stories sold 640 copies at £2 each. So minus all the percentages, it's dinner in the West End. So that was that. No one can find them. No one can pay for them and no one can download them. So the net isn't going to compete with books. It's hugely overhyped. The market isn't there.'

However, a contract's a contract and Forsyth kept to his and delivered the rest of his quintet for the Internet before preparing the stories for hardback release in September 2001 under the title *The Veteran*.

Although the idea of E books was novel enough, the public was not behind it in a big way. Indeed Dickens and a few other writers used to sell their wares in serialisation, as I reminded Forsyth, who told me, 'Yes but there's one important thing about that, those magazines are no longer in circulation. Gone are the days when you paid your sixpence and you received your latest Sherlock Holmes short story, or your latest episode of *Bleak House*. And that's mainly because life is lived at a much faster pace nowadays, people don't want to wait a whole week – or however long – for the next instalment of a story.'

Although the mechanics of E Books was not that successful a process for Forsyth, Ed Victor (Forsyth's agent) told *The Bookseller* in February 2001, '[Forsyth found the process of writing his E book] a mirror image of a conventional publishing deal. Freddie likes good editing . . . he's a believer in improving things.'

It would also be unfair to run down Online Originals for the way the book fared, because they did try hard in turning out a professional product for Forsyth, as Ed Victor also advised *The Bookseller*: 'They had a freelance editor working for them who Freddie thought was terrific, who did really good editing, quite rigorous. They treated him well.'

If anything, the timing was slightly wrong for buying books through the Internet. Indeed, there are still some technical problems with E purchasing, perhaps too many different computer packages at present causing software conflicts. Some streamlining is necessary before the Internet becomes more user-friendly.

Also, books are an ancient wisdom, loved by the materialist. The person who enjoys paying their £15 for a hardback book to sit proudly on their bookshelf would not be content to pay basically the same price for an oversized black and white print-out, or alternatively, an unattractive computer disc. Packaging has always been a major part of any advertising campaign, as rock star David Bowie observed on the advent of the pop video: 'The eyes are much more hungry than the ears.'

Quintet was a brave attempt by Forsyth – and Online Originals – to push back the boundaries of buying books through the net. It was a valiant effort but some more marketing work – and consumer support – needs to be forthcoming before this way of purchasing becomes successful. There is no doubt that it will, but a lot of hard work has to be done first.

18

The Veteran

You can live in a bloody great city like London, with millions of people all around you, but if you keep yourself to yourself, as he must have done, no one ever knows you exist.

The Veteran

WHEN IT was announced that Forsyth's Internet stories were to be released as an anthology (*Bookseller*, 1 June 2001) his legions of fans – and not least of all his agent and publisher – breathed a sigh of relief. At last Forsyth was *slowly* returning to his former style: quality modern day thrillers.

The book's title – *The Veteran* – could describe Forsyth himself. He had by now been a successful novelist for 30 years and was beginning to believe that it was nearly time to call it a day; as Lord Janner said to me in March 2001: 'Frederick Forsyth has told me that he has decided to write no more novels. Alas.'

Forsyth was a veteran novelist. He had achieved so much there was little else to add. Well, apart from *Draco* (see Chapter Nineteen) but that novel was conceived as a short story first; the idea just grew from there.

The Veteran was a more rounded anthology than *No Comebacks*. The stories were a little longer – and ostensibly more detailed – than their earlier counterparts.

To expand upon this analogy a little more, *No Comebacks* presented the quick fix: ten short stories – seemingly unconnected – all with a pay-off ending. However, the stories in *The Veteran* – especially the title story – have a real 'keep them guessing' feel about them, so typically Forsyth. So he worked better with a broader canvas, something nearing novella length, not unlike *The Shepherd*.

In order to analyse Forsyth – and *The Veteran* – a little more closely, I would like to look at the four shorter stories in the anthology in more detail, starting with the title story itself.

> It was the owner of the small convenience store on the corner who saw it all. At least, he said he did.
>
> *The Veteran*

Forsyth starts in a good storytelling mode but perhaps a little less formal than what we are used to. Despite this, the reader is instantly introduced to the more seedy side of life: a man is mugged and beaten into a coma. Suddenly the blacks and greys of a suburban jungle cascade upon us:

> By 1996 the warren of passages, underpasses and alleys that linked the grim residential blocks were crusted with filth, slick with urine and came alive only at night when gangs of local youths, unemployed and unemployable, roamed their manor to 'score' from the area drug peddlers.
>
> *The Veteran*

Forsyth paints an ugly picture of the youth of today and soon locates this teenage hell in 'North East quadrant (of London) where a stranger is unwise to roam'.

Unfortunately – in Forsyth's story – a stranger has roamed and therefore paid the consequences. The beating is brutal.

From here a story of police and legal procedure unfolds: Mr Veejay Patel has seen the assault through his shop window and like a good citizen he instantly calls the emergency services. The police and an ambulance quickly arrive and many questions are soon asked. Who was the stranger assaulted? Where did he come from? As he was an old man, what was he doing out in that part of town so late?

Forsyth posts so many intriguing questions into the reader's mind, it is impossible to put the book to one side.

> The police search units do an unlovely job. Dressed in heavy-duty overalls and protective gloves, their task is to search the areas around crime scenes for clues.
>
> *The Veteran*

As we have come to appreciate, Forsyth enjoys researching procedures, from the formalities of security procedures in the Ministry of Defence (see *The Fourth Protocol* – Chapter Eleven), through to the day-to-day routine of the Metropolitan Police and the CID. *The Veteran* is simply drenched with this kind of detail but it doesn't hinder the story, it complements it. The reader is completely drawn into the core of the case.

But is there much of a case?

Mr Patel has seen everything. He's looked at some mug shots at the local police station and instantly identified the two men who assaulted the old man. They were known criminals, arrested and, incredibly, one was found to have blood on his T-shirt – the victim's blood.

It's an open and shut case. Or is it?

> Rarely is a detective blessed with a case wrapped up like a Christmas parcel simply being delivered to his desk.
>
> *The Veteran*

Despite all the threads seemingly tied up, Forsyth manages to keep you thinking; and thinking such things as 'this is far too pat'.

He knows it. So he changes tack completely, focusing his attention on the man in the coma. We still know very little about him. The police are obviously keen to speak to him but he is 'still far away in his own world'.

Interestingly, it is here that Forsyth really makes a departure from his usual style. He allows the reader into the mind of the comatose victim, glimpsing snapshot memories. And suddenly – through this exclusive insight – the story becomes even more intriguing.

> The Hon. James Vansittart QC stood in the window bay of his chambers and gazed out across the gardens towards the Thames. He was fifty-two and one of the most notable and successful barristers at the London Bar.
>
> *The Veteran*

A famous barrister decides to get involved and suddenly the reader finds himself immersed in a court case. From here we can draw a parallel to *Privilege* in *No Comebacks*. But although a very good story, *Privilege* fails to deliver as many twists and turns in its plot, mainly due to its length.

The Veteran is an excellent story that doesn't give up its secrets until the very end. It was the obvious title story for the anthology because of its depth and complexity. However, as Forsyth told me during a telephone conversation in May 2001: 'My publisher wanted to call the anthology *The Veteran* because it would be in uniform with two of my previous books, *The Negotiator* and *The Deceiver*.' So a commercial decision eventually dictated the title. However, I pointed out that the original Internet title (*Quintet*) was an excellent one. Forsyth told me: 'Yes, I liked it too. But I'm happy with the decision to change it.'

> You must understand, Signore, that these were terrible times
> for the holy Catholic Church. Even I must say so; it had
> grown venal and corrupt on too long a diet of privilege,
> power and wealth.
>
> *The Miracle*

Originally released on the Internet in November 2000, *The
Miracle* took the reader down to the ancient brick alleyways of
Siena, Tuscany, a beautiful medieval city where the sun is 'a
hammer in the sky'.

The story: a wealthy American tourist rushes his wife along the
uneven cobblestones in order to see the start of the famous Palio
horserace.

Unfortunately, the lady stumbles and twists her ankle.
Concerned, her husband escorts her to a nearby bench to inspect
the injury.

A stranger wanders by and offers to bandage the ankle. The
couple are taken in by the man's charm and like a Ulama from the
middle east (the wise man who sits under a tree reciting stories),
the man begins to recite the story of *The Miracle* that happened
in the very place they sat during the last days of the Second
World War.

Although the lady feels better half way through the stranger's
story and encourages her husband to continue – to the race – he
remains mesmerised by the story and misses the race in order to
hear its conclusion. And what a tale it is: of bravery, compassion,
duty and corruption. A story about a vision of a girl long dead,
who comes back to aid the dying and injured troops stationed in
Siena during the last days of the Second World War.

The Miracle is Forsyth re-visiting some of his more familiar
themes. The final twist is greed and man's lust for material
wealth. As this theme itself surfaces in many of Forsyth's novels,
one cannot help but speculate that he too is a very material

person. Not so, as he told me in September 2000: 'I am not a collector. I don't have many possessions. I have enough for my needs.'

It is only when we talk of material things that we find he has no love of them but is intrigued by people who do, as he told me candidly in March 2000: 'If I ever wrote the story of my life I would be up a gum tree. I don't have many photographs of me with celebrities. Some people do. It's all me, me, me. Me with Thatcher, me with Clinton and so on. I don't have any of that.'

The Miracle is a beautifully told story, not dissimilar to Roald Dahl's uncanny tales in his anthology *Someone Like You*. Indeed there are many similarities between the writers: their love of exotic locales, their love of flying, their passion for Bordeaux wines and their bewilderment of where they actually get their ideas from, as Dahl told me in 1981: 'I never really know where my ideas come from and why they are so popular.' Forsyth, almost word for word, told me the same thing in March 2001. He also mentioned his 'bewilderment' in print, in the Preface to his first anthology of short stories, *The Novels of Frederick Forsyth* published by Hutchinson in 1978: 'My first novel, *The Day of the Jackal*, must remain, I believe, one of the most accidental novels ever written. For this reason its almost immediate and continuing success is all the more bewildering – to me if to no one else.'

Perhaps it is because Forsyth and Dahl started out with radically different careers from novel writing – both pilots – their modesty stems from the question 'how the hell did I get here in the first place?'

They left the courtyard and turned down the alley to the sound of the celebrations in the streets beyond.

The Miracle

When one reads *The Miracle*, it becomes plain that Forsyth

wandered along the same alleyways in Siena where the bulk of the story takes place, as he confirmed to me in February 2000: 'I was walking down an alleyway in Siena and asked myself: what have the bricks around me seen over the past 600 years? Some strange people must have been down this alleyway.

'I then came across this little courtyard...and the idea came to me about a young girl who came back. And I thought no, I can't do that. So I pursued a different route.'

The Miracle – for me – doesn't have the most breathtaking twist at its conclusion but it is one of those stories you return to. The historical detail is captivating and there is some wonderful imagery too. Add to this the fact that the two American tourists – the protagonists – are, eventually, endearing, you have a very subtle and quite different story from Forsyth.

> In more than thirty years driving large aluminium tubes around the world for British Airways he had seen over seventy major cities, most of them capitals, and the original appetite had long faded.
>
> *The Citizen*

The Citizen is a story about a night flight from Bangkok to London. The pilot is an old hand (see above quote) and the flight appears to be quite routine. However, strange things are afoot. Assignations in the half-darkness and mysterious messages to the captain (Fallon), all these aspects cause concern. London is informed and suddenly the reader is guessing who is the guilty party aboard aircraft Speedbird One Zero.

The Citizen is based upon a simple idea – just a normal flight – but Forsyth twists and turns the plot in such a tenacious manner one tends to overlook this fact.

When all the characters climb aboard the flight, the story takes on all the key elements of a great whodunit. People from all walks of life are assembled (through First Class, Club Class and World Travel Class). They settle into their seats and embark upon their journey. And you are right there beside them.

> While the First Officer ran through the first of the five separate lists of checks, the Before Start checks, Fallon glanced at the load sheet which he would have to sign when all the luggage was confirmed aboard...
>
> *The Citizen*

It is here that the reader – with a wry smile – goes through the take-off with the passengers, as Forsyth presents all the procedures of the manoeuvre, enhancing the reader's anticipation of something sinister ahead. However, this is no disaster movie and Forsyth – in one of his best ever short stories – remains to the end, one step ahead.

> The finest Columbian cocaine would exchange at three to one; six kilograms of coke against two of a Thai White.
>
> *The Citizen*

The Citizen is essentially a story about drug smuggling but it is not in any way old-fashioned. Forsyth's 'modern' characters and eye for detail keep this story firmly contemporary.

However, a general observation about the stories in *The Veteran* is: most teenagers seem to be untrustworthy. This isn't a recurring theme in Forsyth's writing, although it can be detected in more than one story in *The Veteran*.

My final point about *The Citizen* is to do with the second paragraph of the story:

> Thirty years ago, bright-eyed and bushy-tailed, with the two rings of a Junior First Officer gleaming new on each sleeve,

he had relished the far and foreign places... he had explored
the nightlife of Europe and the USA, taken the offered tours
of the temples and shrines of the Far East. Now, he just
wanted to get home to his house near Dorking.'

The Citizen

Although Forsyth is describing the personality of Captain Fallon
here, he could also be describing himself.

Throughout his life (as we have seen in this book), Forsyth has
lived, worked and visited many places all around the world. But
over the past five years at least, he has slowed down a little. He's
more content to live at a slower pace and enjoy the British
country life. After all, he grew up in a rural town – not surprising
then that he should choose to return to a rural setting.

Quite early in the month the sensation hit the art world.

The Art of the Matter

In May 2001, Forsyth announced that he was to auction his
collection of Lowry paintings because their 'novelty has worn
off'.

This action enforces his claim that he is not a very materialistic
person. However, he did also state that another reason for selling
the paintings was that his wife 'was getting bored with them'.

Regardless of the reasons for selling, the announcement of nine
of Lowry's matchless painting going under the hammer at
Christie's caused more than a ripple of excitement in the art
world.

The paintings were expected to fetch over £1 million when
auctioned in June 2001 and, indeed, the final figure achieved was
£1.7 million.

However, it could be thought that Forsyth's decision to sell his
Lowrys was a direct result of having written a short story about

the art world in December 2000 (and published on the Internet February 2001).

The Art of the Matter is a whimsical little story about an out of work actor Trumpington Gore, 'Trumpy'; as Forsyth told me in March 2001: 'The story is about scams in the art world and is meant to be funny.

'We start with a little man (Trumpy) who wants to sell his last possession, a grubby old oil painting. However, he doesn't know that the oil happens to be a masterpiece. So this out of work actor – who just happens to be a human chameleon – tries to sell his painting.'

Trumpy receives just over £5,000 for the painting which he is delighted with but that is only a fraction of what the painting is actually worth. He has been ripped off and is told as much by a former employee of the gallery (the House of Darcy) he sold it to.

> The painting, tempera on poplar board, was much as the artist would have finished it. The colours glowed as fresh as when they were applied over five hundred years before.
>
> The Virgin Mary sat, gazing upwards, entranced, as the Archangel Gabriel brought her the Annunciation that she would soon bear in her womb the Son of God.
>
> *The Art of the Matter*

Peregrine Slade is the man who has cheated Trumpy (Slade is the Vice-Chairman and Chief Executive Officer of the House of Darcy). His reasons for doing so are to earn promotion within the company and to keep his extravagant wife in the style she demands. She is the daughter of a duke and would not take second best.

However, the former employee of the House of Darcy – Benjamin 'Benny' Evans – was sacked by Slade and had worked out what he was up to. That was when he decided to visit Trumpy whereupon the two of them could work their revenge upon the Vice-Chairman of Darcy.

With the help of Benny's girlfriend Julie Day (an odd looking youngster who is a computer whiz) they become a formidable team. Benny knows the art trade and Trumpy can't wait to get into character to pull off one of the greatest scams in the art world.

> He had slicked-back thin black hair and gold-rimmed glasses. He was two inches taller, in a beautifully cut, but rented, pinstripe suit, Thomas Pink shirt and Brigade of Guards tie. He turned and walked straight past the waiting girl.
>
> 'Damned good auction, what?' He could not resist it. 'See that American fella got his piece.'
>
> He nodded towards the door behind him and strode on. The girl kept staring at the lavatory door.
>
> *The Art of the Matter*

One could picture *The Art of the Matter* as a classic Ealing comedy, both humorous and ingenious. When Forsyth speaks of the story and his loveable character of Trumpington Gore, he can't resist the temptation to fall into character himself and recite the above quote in his best 'brigade' accent.

Although the sale of his Lowrys was coincidental to the publication of the story, it was in no way intentional. However, if *The Art of the Matter* was a novel by itself, the sale of the painting would have proved to be the most novel of promotion scams imaginable. A shame it wasn't really.

> The girl squatted in the mud and held the torso of the filthy old beggar, but he was dying from his beating. Though such people must have been alive with parasites, stinking of mud

and excrement, she held him in her arms as he died.

The Miracle

The Veteran is an excellent anthology of very different stories. Although they differ greatly from what Forsyth has dealt us before, they all have that unmistakable touch of a complete master at the height of his powers.

19
Enter *Draco*

FORSYTH'S NEXT novel will be called *Draco*. A book that marks a welcome return to the thriller genre. Something he hasn't tackled since his 1996 novel *Icon*.

Draco is typically Forsyth – almost a caricature – an extreme central character, a man who is an isolationist but has a very serious role to play in modern day society.

In February 2001, Forsyth advised me, '*Draco* is just an idea at the moment. I haven't started researching it yet.'

But what is the novel based upon? He explained, 'It's based on the concept that in America they still have bounty hunters.' Images of Clint Eastwood's Man With No Name suddenly come to mind but as Forsyth is keen to point out: 'The bounty hunter, in America, is a perfectly legitimate profession, usually carried out by licensed private investigators.'

Forsyth then compounded this idea with a little bit of American law to develop the story, as he explained: 'In a state in America, a man is charged with a serious offence and he secures a bail-bonding for a quarter of a million, and he quits the jurisdiction. Now, except for federal offences, state jurisdiction ends at the state border. So a man charged with an offence in Texas, and seeking refuge in neighbouring New Mexico, cannot be extradited. Well, he can, but it takes time. And quite possibly, it would be turned down.'

So after observing this piece of American law, a story began to take shape. 'The bail bondsman is set to lose his quarter of a million. And supposing you have a man who refused to accept, never mind state boundaries, but international boundaries. And there is this character that has done something truly horrendous in American jurisdiction, made a lot of money out of it, and spends the rest of his life in luxury in the Dominican Republic, or somewhere. But of course, there is *Draco* – and if you pay him – he will bring him back for you.'

Forsyth looked at the world of high finance to examine some of the multi-million-pound scams that go on. But, as we all know, there are worse villains out there. 'There are people who have a far more serious pedigree than bent financiers,' Forsyth told me. 'People who kill, torture and rape. They escape. And just imagine, a father of a girl who was gang raped, who spends the rest of her life in a coma. To the father, it's not good enough that this person has got away. He wants justice. He says, "I have the money, I want the bastard back." And *Draco* will go and bring him back.'

It's a powerful concept and an out-and-out thriller, a genre Forsyth said he would never return to. I asked him why he decided to write thrillers again, especially after putting out such diverse works as *The Phantom of Manhattan* and *Quintet* (*The Veteran*). He said: 'Yes, I've gone back to what I said I was giving up – the harder, more masculine type of novel.'

Although *The Veteran* received a lot of exposure and sales figures of the hardback would obviously be good, did the disappointing sales figure of *The Phantom of Manhattan* persuade him to go back to the thriller? He explained: 'It didn't match my thrillers in sales figures. Both my agent and my publisher said: "Come on, Freddie, stop messing about." So I gave them both what they wanted.' And the general public as well, but *Draco* had been bubbling away for a couple of years before Forsyth started to write it down.

The novel was first heard of on the Internet as part of the anthology *Quintet*. In mid-December 2000, after the release of the first three stories on-line, it was announced that the next two in the anthology would be 'Art of the Matter' and 'Draco'.

In February 2001, when I discussed *Quintet* with Forsyth, he gave me a breakdown of each story in the anthology. But when we came to the last story – which I presumed to be 'Draco' – he told me about 'Whispering Wind' instead which I had never heard of. Once we had discussed that story, (the fifth and longest story in the anthology), I then asked him about 'Draco' and was told, 'That will be my next novel.' So the idea expanded from a short story into a novel approximately 500 pages long.

Despite the departure he promised – and fulfilled – after writing *Icon* (*The Phantom of Manhattan*, *Quintet*, and even a large helping hand in this, his first biography-type project), Forsyth returned to the genre that has served him so well over the past 30 years: the thriller.

Draco is a killer of an idea and will prove to be yet another international bestseller from the Forsyth pen, although as he told me in February 2001, he will have to answer to his critics: 'I'm going to be heavily criticised for returning to the thriller, especially after saying that I never would.'

However, if you're good at something, why ignore it?

20
The World of Frederick Forsyth

FREDERICK FORSYTH'S novels are peopled with a colourful array of traitors, killers, soldiers, mercenaries and civil servants. A world that on the surface seems to 'toe the party line', but in truth, pokes fun at the 'old school tie'.

Politics – that international language – is vast and intricate and Frederick Forsyth has always explored thought-provoking scenarios. His speculation may not always be correct, but because his work is often so plausible, one tends to believe that one day it might. For example, we are aware that the Russian economy was not plunged into chaos in 1999 – and headed by a ruthless dictator – as depicted in *Icon*, but the book is still a captivating read and – not unlike *Nineteen Eighty Four* (another book constrained by a particular point in time) – gives pause for thought.

Following a similar line, we observe Forsyth's 'fears' of Communists winning general elections (see *The Fourth Protocol*) are unfounded. However, *The Fourth Protocol* is one of his very best thrillers.

From the outset, Forsyth found a voice and a highly innovative style. Books like *The Day of the Jackal*, *The Odessa File* and *The Dogs of War* set a brand new trend in the thriller genre (as novelist Ian Rankin says, 'Frederick Forsyth has a lot to answer for'). By the time aspiring writers began to imitate Forsyth's style, he had already moved on, blending more political awareness into his stories; *The Devils Alternative* and *The Fourth Protocol* are good examples. From there, we witnessed the Berlin Wall come down and the Cold War end, but instead of hanging up his boots, Forsyth showed us that there was so much else going on in the world with diverse fiction such as *The Negotiator* and *The Fist of God*.

If one looks closely, it becomes clear how Forsyth's work has changed over the years. Obviously nostalgia freaks will always go to *The Day of the Jackal* when asked what their favourite book is. There is nothing wrong with this of course, the book is wonderful, but it should be appreciated how much research and quality 'thriller writing' and research went into later novels such as *The Fist of God* and *Icon*.

The Phantom of Manhattan was not his greatest achievement by any stretch of the imagination but it was a brave step, clearly showing that Forsyth could write a story in a totally different genre – the gothic novel.

Quintet was really the struggle to refrain from writing another thriller; however, the idea to write an E book in the most accessible way – a set of short stories – did present another dimension to his work and give a second – and much awaited – anthology of short fiction (*The Veteran*).

However, the leopard doesn't change its spots too much, and *Draco* is Forsyth's return to the out-and-out thriller novel. We could criticise him for that, but, perhaps, waiting to see Forsyth go full circle, back to the genre where he is best suited, is what we were all waiting for. Perhaps after a five-year break from the genre he can return with batteries recharged and deliver what his public expects: quality thrillers, meticulously researched. However, it is quite possible that after *Draco* Forsyth will retire from writing fiction and concentrate more on politics. It is a theory that has often been speculated upon.

Frederick Forsyth has not been the most prolific of writers in the world – this is mostly due to all that research he does – and the time he dedicates to other pursuits, including public speaking.

He freely admits that he is 'a commercial writer', which is why he has so many international locations in his books; so his fans the world over can identify with certain stories, or aspects of those stories.

Forsyth will spend time discussing political pressures and international relationships – from his own Conservative point of view – especially in Cold War books like *The Deceiver* and to an extent *The Fourth Protocol* and *Icon*.

However, there is a formality and etiquette to the world of Frederick Forsyth, the way he deals with real-life characters in his books and the political eco-systems of foreign countries. If this didn't happen, he wouldn't enjoy a worldwide readership for what has been 30 successful years. This proves – if proof is needed – that Frederick Forsyth's winning formula for writing international thrillers is just a matter of protocol: thought-provoking stories based upon plausible political situations.

The home run was always his favourite. In more than thirty years . . . he had seen over seventy major cities, most of them capitals, and the original apetite had faded.

Thirty years ago, bright-eyed and bushy-tailed . . . he had relished the far and foreign places.

The Citizen
Frederick Forsyth

Part Three
The Forsyth Legacy

The Forsyth Legacy

THE FINAL part of this book is split into four sections. One: an interview with Forsyth's agent Ed Victor entitled Mixing Business and Pleasure. Two: an uncut interview with Frederick Forsyth himself, which explores his thoughts and opinions in a succinct and open way. Three: a detailed film guide, noting all the major movie and TV adaptations of his work, including interview segments with Edward Fox, Sir Derek Jacobi and Forsyth himself. Four: a detailed bibliography of Forsyth's novels and other miscellaneous works.

My intention through these four distinct chapters is to show other aspects of Forsyth's character so far unexplored in this book.

Mixing Business and Pleasure:
An Interview with Ed Victor

'It's like listening to a great violin player.'

Ed Victor

WHAT FOLLOWS is a short interview with Frederick Forsyth's agent Ed Victor. The interview not only shows the way Forsyth conducts himself professionally, it also illustrates how a successful business relationship can be formed from a friendship.

When did you first meet Frederick Forsyth?
'I first met Freddie in the 70s. I had a very strange book offered to me – which was eventually published – written by a man who claimed to have spied for Winston Churchill as a 15-year-old child during the Second World War.

'It was a very intriguing story but I had no way of checking it out. So I got in touch with Freddie to see if he would like to write something (a faction novel based upon the idea). He was living in Ireland at the time and I went over there. I spent the afternoon with him and talked about the book over a cup of tea. However, he passed the historical details off as fantasy, which was very discouraging to me. He was very polite about it, very business-like. Even though he was writing at the highest level a young man

could write at, he was not arrogant. He was terrific, but he was
very negative about my project.'

How did the friendship develop?
'Over the years I would see him socially – at parties. And then I
began to see him more when he met his [second] wife Sandy. I
knew her, so things went on from there.

   'About five years ago, he asked to see me and he told me that
his current agent – who he had been fiercely loyal to since the
early 70s – was retiring. He was very fond of her but didn't want
to stay on with the company who took over, so that's when I
became his agent.'

*The relationship has been a good one, but Forsyth has told me
that you have asked him to write thrillers again, rather than
concentrate on other types of writing such as* The Phantom of
Manhattan, *is that true?*
'Yes and I'm pleased that he is going back to the thriller. You see,
it's like listening to a great violin player, enjoying every little
thing about the music, relishing every single performance, then
suddenly finding that he wants to play the trombone.

   'Now you may find that he can play the trombone very well
but you want him to go back to playing the violin because that
is what he is best at.'

*Where do you see him going in the future? Do you think he will
give up the novel and concentrate on politics – he does have
some very strong views?*
'Well, I would like to see him continue with his writing, which he
is for the time being. However, he is very passionate about
politics, but I'm not sure where he will take that interest in the
future.

Do you think he is good for the Conservative Party?
'Yes I do. But I don't think he will pursue politics, certainly not at the moment. His next full-length novel [*Draco*] is based upon a very powerful idea and he has his work cut out for the foreseeable future on that.'

Frederick Forsyth:
Thoughts and Opinions

> I was born the son of two shopkeepers and raised therefore
> to the idea that our police are wonderful.
>
> *Frederick Forsyth*

ONE WEEKEND in September 2000, I interviewed Frederick
Forsyth for a police-related magazine, edited by a friend of mine.

I met Forsyth in the bar of the Langham Hilton, opposite
BBC radio headquarters. What I didn't realise at the time was
that he had just finished a broadcast and was still very much in
transmit mode.

The following segment is presented to the reader raw. In
other words, it's an honest transcript from my taped interview.
I have resisted the temptation to edit, tone down or, in any way,
shape what was said. My reason for this is solely because the
interview – as it stands – shows a side of Forsyth so far
unexplored in this book.

We know Frederick Forsyth to be a bestselling novelist and
a very well respected journalist, but he is also a very effective
public speaker, with clear views and rationale. The following
complements this latter side through subjects I – briefly –
bring up.

The following speaks volumes about Forsyth's political and moral stance and needs no further analysis from me. It stands by itself as a wonderful piece of, well, rhetoric!

What do you think of the police force today?
'I was born the son of two shopkeepers and raised therefore to the idea that our police are wonderful. My father was good friends with a couple of inspectors at the local station, and civility and courtesy between members of the police force and the public was taken for granted. It was also taken for granted that the broad mass of the British public were tax-paying, law-abiding people, so therefore the police were their protectors against crime, and not their persecutors.

'Now what I think has changed – and I say this with the deepest sadness – is that that perception has been eroded, principally over the past decade. And I fear that, although 99.9 per cent of police officers will admit that the job is undoable, they could not exist without public co-operation. I don't just mean when a child goes missing, I mean co-operation at every level. Because if you have the public on side, you have – when you need them – some 20 million detectives. People are prepared to keep their eyes open, their ears open, check in with the police, note a car number, keep the police informed, and without that co-operation policing would be impossible.

'I think I see a waning of the natural – native – enthusiasm for the police among the middle class in Britain, and of the law-abiding working class. I'm sorry to see this, but I think it's happening because of political correctness, because of the perceived ineffectuality in combating crime that affects people – I don't mean parking on a yellow line or speeding in a 30-mile zone – I mean having your house burgled, having your car trashed, being beaten up on the street – that affects people badly. So there does seem to be a lack of confidence.'

Do you think TV is presenting the police in a negative light?
'No, I don't think it is. You see *The Bill* and broadly speaking one empathises with them. Broadly speaking, they do solve cases; I wonder if that is the experience of every police station, let alone in inner London.

'All this started after the war with a film called *The Blue Lamp*. I remember it very well. It was a solidly pro-police film. We went from there to *Dixon of Dock Green*. Wonderful. There was old Dixon – "evening all" – who was the neighbourhood bobby, he was clearly avuncular, and even the youngsters were on our side. We then moved on to *Z Cars*, and again, overwhelmingly sympathetic characters.

'Today we're looking at *Crimewatch* and programmes like that which get enormous support from the public. Why, therefore, is there this perception about rural policing that the police aren't doing their job, that they are not getting results? I think that there has been a breakdown, because the more effort the police put behind community policing and addressing meetings, the less effect it has. It worries me, and I think it is down to things like the McPherson Report, which I profoundly disagreed with, slagging off the police all the time as the enemy of the people, the enemy of ethnic minorities – in my opinion they're not and never were – that they are institutionally racist. Yes, there will be some; but also in the legal and journalistic profession there will be some. But despite all that, it is never said that policemen who are corrupt are a tiny minority, policemen who forge evidence are a tiny minority, policemen who create confessions or beat confessions out of people are a tiny minority, and the police who are racially antagonistic are a tiny minority, and the bulk are trying to do a damn good job, in extremely difficult circumstances. Now, that's not pointed out, because in essence, I think, incumbent government is hostile to the police, and that I don't like, because it was never like that before.'

What about police who are instructed to work in political situations, such as policing duties in Kosovo after the conflict?
'I obviously listen to all the opinions. I listened to (the eminent military historian) Corelli Barnett who said we should never have gone near the damn place under any circumstances – no matter what the Serbs did to the Kosovans – right through to the Blairites who said that it was one of the most wonderful things that ever happened, and what a marvellous outcome we achieved.

'I don't take either view. I'm afraid I take the view that we reached the point, after the dismal failure of the Rambouillet talks, where what Milosevic was doing to the Kosovans was moving from persecution to pogrom to genocide, and our choice was: do we turn around and face away, stare at the Atlantic, the clouds, stare at whatever we want to stare at while an entire people – likeable or not – it doesn't matter, loveable or not – we didn't know – are subjected to genocide, because that was his intent? You don't have to kill anybody to conduct genocide. If you chase people from their home in winter, into a wilderness of snow and ice, that's genocide and that's what he was preparing to do. We knew it. We had proof beyond any reasonable doubt through our intelligence agencies. That was his game plan, to actually ethnically cleanse the whole of the Kosovan province. To have turned our backs? I don't think we could have done. Having said that, I think the whole operation was a big cock-up from start to finish.'

I think – throughout history – we (the British) have had a tendency to get too involved, don't you think?
'Well, we didn't have any choice in the Second World War. Adolf Hitler was a bit bigger than Milosevic. We didn't get involved in Rwanda. We knew genocide was going on. We accepted that it was simply too far away. We had no air bridge. Even if we landed there, nobody was in uniform. This was an internecine side massacre and it was decided not to go in. We

didn't go into the Congo, even though the war there still goes on. Brutal, bloody and foul – as all wars are. We did decide to go into Sierra Leone because I think the assessment was that there was a reasonable chance of having an effect, not simply that we would be swallowed up into some bottomless pit of jungle warfare.

'There are times that we have to take a position and that position must be partly practical, partly moral. I don't believe in the Ethical Foreign Policy of Mr Cook, it's a load of rubbish. One can have a humane foreign policy or a policy that attempts to be humane, but you've got to have the practicalities in mind, for example, we cannot invade China to liberate Tibet. We never invaded Indonesia to free East Timor, because they're too far away, and without a radical change of circumstances, we would – quite frankly – be wiped out. So one has to be practical, as much as to say "this is feasible, this is not feasible". Both may be genocide, to intervene in one may be feasible, however, the other may not be. And when we can't, despite the horrible images that appear on television, we have to say we can't do anything about it, we can't be a universal gendarme. Now and again we think we can make a difference, then we try. That would happen under a Conservative regime or a Labour regime because it's part of the British nature to try to help people, if we can.'

Do you think the Labour Party has a tendency to mess things up more than the Conservative Party?
'You mean like Suez? No. Very simply, it's not a question of messing, it's interfering. Yes, the Labour Party has a much greater capacity to interfere, the presumption that it is the holder of some holy grail of wisdom, that it knows more about generalship than generals, it knows more about business than businessmen, it knows more about banks than bankers, or about farming than farmers and so on. It certainly knows more about

educating children than teachers or parents, if you believe it. And, I think, this temptation to play Alexandra the Great in the Balkans was simply too much. Having said that, the interference was negative and counter-productive, it was indeed disastrous. It proved – if proof was needed – that you cannot run a war on the basis that every decision has to go to 19 NATO councillors, and that each council member has to then consult with its home government, and each home government says yea or nay. You can't run a war like that, and I hope that NATO will never run another war that way, the way Kosovo was run, because it can't be done.

'I think NATO got away with a near miracle, but the final outcome was down to a fat old Russian, who told Milosevic to his face that Russia, the protector of Serbia, would pull the rug out if he didn't compromise and settle, that's what brought an end to it. It wasn't the bombing, the killing of soldiers, because virtually no killing of soldiers took place.'

Some of Frederick Forsyth's speeches can be downloaded from the Internet nowadays, and all have their own shelf-life like any other political or after dinner conversation.

What I love about the 'thoughts and opinions' you have just read is that this was not a rehearsed piece. It was a string of spontaneous answers to questions asked in the interview room. It was in no way planned. Forsyth speaks with confidence and knowledge and that in turn speaks volumes about the man's depth and political awareness.

Frederick Forsyth Film Guide

Writing a script is nothing like writing a book.

Frederick Forsyth

WHAT FOLLOWS is a detailed guide to the various film and TV adaptations of Frederick Forsyth's novels and short stories.

The chapter opens with a brief interview with Forsyth, where he explains the frustrations of converting a novel to film but clearly stating what his favourite – and least favourite – movie adaptations are.

Actors Edward Fox and Sir Derek Jacobi then reminisce about their time working on two of the best film adaptations of Forsyth novels: *The Day of the Jackal* and *The Odessa File*. This is followed by detailed cast and crew breakdowns for all the various film and TV adaptations.

Frederick Forsyth discusses the movie adaptations of his novels, both the ones he likes and those he doesn't.
'Five out of ten of my novels have been turned into movies. My favourite is still *The Day of the Jackal*. I've seen it about 15 times, which is very unusual for me. Fred Zinnemann directed it. He directed *High Noon*. A master of his trade. Just before *The*

Day of the Jackal he worked on *A Man For All Seasons*.

'The other film adaptations of my work I acknowledge are: *The Odessa File*, *The Dogs of War*, *The Fourth Protocol* and *The Deceiver*, but I think that I still prefer the first the most – *The Day of the Jackal*.'

You've actually taken a role in film-making yourself with The Fourth Protocol?

'I have become involved in the films. And indeed, became co-executive producer – with Michael Caine – on *The Fourth Protocol*, which Caine starred in. I wasn't that happy with the final product, but I don't think authors ever are.

'The making of a film and what works on screen is so radically different to what works on paper. An author is different to a director. An author thinks, "I can see something in my mind's eye, put that down on paper and put it into the reader's mind, maybe." There you get belief, and the reader turns the page and you find out what happens next. That's not the same with films. You have full colour, actor expressions, body language. Volumes can be said without a word being spoken. You can have a scene where all you see is two street signs and the look on an actor's face, and by all of that you realise the character is in the wrong place. Now, I would have to spend about a page and a half explaining that, but that happens on film in about eight seconds which is why writing for films is very specialised.

'Writing a script is nothing like writing a book. And a director is nothing like an author. This is why films seem to have nothing to do with the books they represent, because the director has a completely different vision to the writer, and that's simply because he wants to make a good film.'

There are occasions however, when the original story is completely ignored. I'm thinking here of the movie starring Bruce Willis and Richard Gere entitled The Jackal.

'The movie called *The Jackal* is a disgrace. Universal – who I'll never work with again – simply happened to own the title of my story *The Day of the Jackal*. And they had an original script without a title. It had nothing to do with De Gaulle and the OAS but it was a story about a professional assassin, that was the only common denominator. And I suppose, in some stupid round table conference, they decided to unearth *The Day of the Jackal*. The only good news is that it was such a turkey of a movie – despite Bruce Willis and Richard Gere being in it who are normally very good – it died within a week, except on video of course.

'So I'm rather pleased to say that sometimes the sins of the movie industry catch up with themselves and they fall flat on their face. But on occasion they also get the magic right. And that is why it is always good to have movies made of your work.'

Actor Edward Fox was picked to play the Jackal in the 1973 movie The Day of the Jackal *because of his excellent theatre credentials. In November 2000, he discussed the shooting of the movie, and the public recognition he still receives for the part to this day.*

'One of the most important turning points in an actor's life is public recognition. I received that with *The Day of the Jackal*. Before "Jackal" I hadn't really done any film work; my working life was based very much in the theatre.

'I knew the movie was going to be big, having been with Fred [Zinnemann] and John Woolf at the beginning of the project, and I never had any doubt that it was going to be a great success too. Not from anything I had to do with it, but simply to do with Fred. He was 65 years old then, but seemed much younger. He had youthful enthusiasm, almost like a 20-year-old would bring to a project.

'I hadn't read the book beforehand, mainly because I don't read books that have just been released, but Fred asked to see me and told me to go away and read Forsyth's novel. I did. Immediately, I had the same reaction to it as everyone else. It was a wonderfully told story.

'The five months I spent making the movie were very memorable. There were some funny moments too. One in particular stands out in my mind: we were shooting the last scene in Paris (where the Jackal makes his attempt on the life of Charles de Gaulle), and I spent a great deal of interesting time designing the disguise I had to wear in order to get near De Gaulle.

'I was practising putting my leg up my backside to look like a one-legged war veteran. I had crutches, specific make-up; it was a lengthy process but nonetheless very interesting. Finally, it looked convincing, not just on camera but in real life. So I was walking down a Paris street and Fred had got some invalid people to make up a crowd of war veterans – quite possibly they were war veterans – and as I was wandering around in this crowd, a woman with one leg came up to me and said, "How did you get yours?" I'm afraid, as she was French, I didn't understand what she had said to me, but Fred roared with laughter, he thought it was absolutely wonderful.

'Since making *The Day of the Jackal* I've become friends with Freddie Forsyth, and I would say he's been a good friend to me. I know him well but I don't see him often. But one feels with Freddie, if he chooses to know you, you're his friend. I would go as far as to say, if one rang Freddie and said, "Look I'm in trouble, can you help?" my bet is that he would say "Leave it with me."

'I read his books and I read his newspaper articles, particularly when he's writing about the European Union. I think he's wonderful on that subject.

'As far as *The Day of the Jackal* is concerned, I don't find it tiresome if people remember me solely for that, because if people remember you for anything you do, you should feel grateful. That is the bottom line truth of the matter, because the object of acting is to make the audience believe you are who you say you are. If people come out of the cinema saying "I believe that man was who he said he was", then you have succeeded. It's all to do with communication and making that communication accessible to the viewer, to the extent where they don't have to strain to understand it.

'However, when you finish a part like the Jackal, you've got to ignore it, breathe deeply, and move on to the next role.'

Sir Derek Jacobi appeared in the first two movie adaptations of Forsyth novels: The Day of the Jackal *and* The Odessa File. *In February 2001, he discussed the making of those films and the importance they had on his film career.*
'I'm particularly fond of *The Day of the Jackal*, because it was the first time that I had been involved in films. And the great thing about Fred Zinnemann was he used actors who had done a great deal of theatre work.

'Edward Fox and I had both started out in a repertory situation and by the time we came to do *The Day of the Jackal* we were ready – as actors – to do it.

'I read the book of *The Day of the Jackal* before I did the film. The first scene I did [as Caron] was in a hotel in Cannes. I was driven up to it in a huge limousine, and that was my first experience of such a thing.'

Your character didn't interact with Edward Fox's in the movie, did he?
'No. I didn't work with Edward Fox in the movie because our parts were completely separate, however I did meet him socially. Actors do get together socially during the shooting of a film, and that's always important.

'One memory does stick out concerning the filming of *The Day of the Jackal* – and I really can't call it a fond memory – I was taken ill on my very first day. A doctor was called in and I was diagnosed with appendicitis. Suddenly, there was a helicopter on standby to rush me to hospital, but fortunately, it was found that I was suffering from food poisoning. It was the fish I had eaten for supper. So the following morning I crawled into make-up and went to work.'

Directly after The Day of the Jackal *you worked on the next film adaptation of a Frederick Forsyth novel* – The Odessa File – *and through what was little more than a cameo role, nearly stole the film.*
'That's very kind of you to say. With *The Odessa File*, I again read the book before I played the part. And because I was playing a German (Klaus Wenzer), I had someone who took me through the part phonetically, so I could get the accent correct.

'I was working with Jon Voight and I remember being a little in awe of him. He was an enormous movie star. He had just done *Midnight Cowboy*, so he was big, big news.

'I do remember one scene where I had to give him an envelope, and we rehearsed it and it went fine, but when we actually came to shoot it, I handed him the envelope and I knew, as an actor, that he had forgotten his lines, but instead of admitting it, he said, "Derek gave me the envelope with his right hand. It threw me. He gave me it with his left in rehearsal."'
Do you look back on those two movies and feel they were important to your film career?
'Yes, I do. Both *The Day of the Jackal* and *The Odessa File* were good for my confidence. They showed that I could work in the medium of films quite comfortably. I was pleased about that, because films reach such an enormous audience. Obviously my heart is in the theatre, but it's good to do the odd film, TV as well.'

FILM AND TV MOVIES

Note: Every effort has been made to offer the most accurate information in this section. However, some minor errors can occur in such a comprehensive list. I apologise in advance if that is the case but if the author and publisher are approached, every effort will be made to correct the error(s) in a future edition of this work.

Please note, only brief plot summaries are included for major motion picture releases, not TV movies.

The Day of the Jackal (1973)
Directed by Fred Zinnemann
Screenplay by Kenneth Ross

Based upon the novel by Frederick Forsyth

Cast:
Edward Fox...The Jackal
Terence Alexander ....Lloyd
Michel Auclair ....Colonel Rolland
Alan Badel...The Minister
Tony Britton ....Inspector Thomas
Denis Carey ....Casson
Adrien Cayla-Legrand...Charles de Gaulle
Cyril Cusack...The Gunsmith
Maurice Denham ....General Colbert
Vernon Dobtcheff...The Interrogator
Jacques François ....Pascal
Olga Georges-Picot ....Denise
Raymond Gérôme ....Flavigny
Barrie Ingham...St. Clair
Derek Jacobi..Caron
Michael Lonsdale ....Detective Lebel
Jean Martin ....Wolenski
Ronald Pickup...The Forger

Eric Porter...Colonel Rodin
Anton Rodgers...Bernard
Delphine Seyrig ....Colette de Montpelier
Donald Sinden...Mallinson
Jean Sorel ....Bastien-Thiry
David Swift ....Montclair
Timothy West ....Berthier

Other cast members:
Bernard Archard, Jacques Alric, Colette Bergé
Edmond Bernard, Gérard Buhr, Philippe Léotard,
Maurice Teynac, Van Doude, Nicolas Vogel,
Edward Hardwicke, Howard Vernon

Produced by
Julien Derode (co-producer)
David Deutsch (co-producer)
John Woolf

Original music by
Georges Delerue

Cinematography by
Jean Tournier

Film Editing by
Ralph Kemplen

Casting
Margot Capelier
Jenia Reissar

Costume Design by
Joan Bridge
Rosine Delamare
Elizabeth Haffenden

Makeup Department
Pierre Berroyer ....makeup artist
Marc Ludovic Paris ....hair stylist (as Marc Paris)
Barbara Ritchie..hair stylist

Production Management
Henri Jaquillard..production manager
John Palmer...production manager

Second Unit Directors or Assistant Directors
Andrew Marton ....second unit director
Louis Pitzele..assistant director
Peter Price ....assistant director

Art Department
René Albouze..property master
Ernest Archer...set designer
Robert Cartwright...set dresser
Pierre Charron ....set dresser
Wally Hill...property master
Willy Holt...set designer

Sound Department
Bob Allen...sound recordist (as Robert Allen)
Gordon K McCallum...dubbing mixer
Nicholas Stevenson ....sound editor

Special Effects
Georges Iaconelli..special effects
Cliff Richardson ....special effects
John Richardson ....special effects

Visual Effects
Wally Veevers...visual effects

Other crew
Guy Delattre ....photographer: second unit

André Domage ....camera operator
Marcel Durham ....assistant editor
Gladys Goldsmith ....continuity
David Harcourt...camera operator
Catherine Prévert ....continuity
John Rosenberg ....script editor
Edmond Séchan.......................................photographer: second unit
Jean Zay ....costume supervisor

Run time: Germany: 145/UK:142
Country: France/UK
Language: English
Colour: Colour (Technicolor)
Sound Mix: Westrex
Certification: Finland: K-16/Norway: 15/Sweden: 15/UK: 15/
USA: PG/West Germany: 16

Storyline: France 1963, the Secret Army Organisation (OAS) have made repeated attempts to assassinate President Charles de Gaulle, but with no success.

As a last resort, they hire a professional assassin, code-named the Jackal, who agrees to kill De Gaulle for half a million dollars. The OAS raise sufficient funds for the hit by a series of robberies. When they have raised the money, they activate the Jackal; but they also activate the French authorities too. A manhunt ensues. The rest of this chase movie details the Jackal's preparations to kill De Gaulle and how he is finally foiled in his plan. Noted outstanding performances from: Edward Fox, Derek Jacobi and Michael Lonsdale.

The Odessa File (1974)
Directed by
Ronald Neame
Screenplay by
Kenneth Ross & George Markstein
Based upon the novel by Frederick Forsyth

Cast:

Jon Voight	Peter Miller
Maximilian Schell	Eduard Roschmann
Maria Schell	Frau Miller
Mary Tamm	Sigi
Derek Jacobi	Klaus Wenzer
Peter Jeffrey	David Porath
Klaus Löwitsch	Gustav Mackensen
Kurt Meisel	Alfred Oster
Hannes Messemer	General Glucks
Garfield Morgan	Israeli General
Shmuel Rodensky	Simon Wiesenthal
Ernst Schröder	Werner Deilman
Gunter Strack	Kunik
Noel Willman	Franz Bayer
Martin Brandt	Marx
Hans Caninenberg	Dr. Ferdinand Schultz
Heinz Ehrenfreund	Shapiro
Alexander Golling	Colonel
Towje Kleiner	Salomon Tauber
Gunter Meisner	General Greifer
Gunnar Möller	Karl Braun
Elisabeth Neumann-Viertel	Frau Wenzer
Christine Wodetzky	Gisela
Werner Bruhns	Hoffmann
Til Kiwe	Medal Shop Proprietor
Georg Marischka	Lawyer
Joachim Dietmar Mues	Wehrmacht Captain
Hans Wypröchtiger	Landlord
Cyril Shaps	Tauber's Voice
Miriam Mahler	Esther Tauber

Produced by
John R. Sloan (co-producer)
John Woolf

Original music by
Andrew Lloyd Webber

Cinematography by
Oswald Morris

Film Editing by
Ralph Kemplen

Casting
Renate Neuchl
Jenia Reissar

Production Design by
Rolf Zehetbauer
Costume Design by
Monika Bauert

Makeup Department
Susi Krause..hair stylist
Raimund Stangl ....makeup artist

Production Management
Pia Arnold ....production supervisor

Second Unit Directors or Assistant Directors
Colin Brewer......................first assistant director (as Colin Brewer)
Wieland Liebske...assistant director

Art Department
Werner Achmann ....construction supervisor
Richard Eglseder...prop buyer
Alois Muehlbauer ....head property (as Alois Muhlbauer)

Sound Department
Derek Ball..sound recordist

Les Hodgson...sound editor
Gordon McCallum ....sound recordist (as Gordon McCallum)
Alan O'Duffy...music recordist

Special Effects
Richard Richtsfeld..special effects

Other crew
Anthony Bowles..conductor
May Capsaskis ....production assistant
Marcel Durham ....assistant editor
Atze Glanert ....second unit camaraman
Leonhard Gmr ....location manager
Freddy Leitensdorfer..................head grip (as Freddy Leitenstorfer)
Dieter Mever...location manager
Osman Ragheb ....dialogue coach
John Rosenberg...script editor
Elaine Schreyeck..continuity
Leonhard Gmuer...location manager
Ille Sievers...wardrobe supervisor
Jimmy Turrell ....camera operator
Simon Wiesenthal..documentary advisor
Also known as:
Akte Odessa, Die (1975) (West Germany)
Fall Odessa, Der (1975) (West Germany)

Runtime: USA:130
Country: UK/West Germany
Language: English
Colour: Colour (Eastmancolor)
Certification: Finland:K-16/Germany:16/Norway:16 (1975)/
Sweden:15/USA:PG

Storyline: Freelance journalist Peter Miller drives home through Hamburg on the evening of 22 November 1963. He follows an ambulance believing that it will lead him to a big story. Unfortunately it doesn't.

Miller only finds that an elderly Jew has gassed himself, rather than a front page headline story. He goes home disappointed but the following day, he is called by a friend at the local police station. Miller meets up with the officer where he is given the dead Jew's diary. It details the atrocities of the Nazi holocaust and the actions of a Camp Commandant by the name of Eduard Roschmann whom the Jew had recently seen in Hamburg.

Suddenly Miller risks everything in order to track down Roschmann. There is clearly more to the dead Jew's diary than meets the eye.

Although its ending is radically different from that of the novel, this is an exceptionally good movie. Noted outstanding performances from Jon Voight, Maximilian Schell, Mary Tamm and Derek Jacobi.

The Dogs of War (1980)
Directed by John Irvin
Screenplay by Gary DeVore and George Malko
Based upon the novel by Frederick Forsyth

Cast:
Christopher Walken...Shannon
Tom Berenger..Drew
Colin Blakely ....North
Hugh Millais..Endean
Paul Freeman ....Derek
Jean-François Stévenin ....Michel
Jobeth Williams...Jessie
Robert Urquhart ....Capt. Lockhart
Winston Ntshona ....Dr. Okoye
Pedro Armendáriz Jr. ....The Major (as Pedro Armendáriz)
Harlan Cary Poe ....Richard
Ed O'Neill..Terry
Ernest Graves..Warner
Kelvin Thomas...The Black Boy
Shane Rimmer...Dr. Oaks
Bruce McLane ....Shop Manager

George W. Harris ....Col. Bobi
David Schofield...Endean's Man
Terence Rigby ....Hackett
Tony Mathews ....Bank Vice President
John Quentin ....Party Guest
Jean-Pierre Kalfon...Benny Lambert
Christopher Malcolm..Baker
Jack Lenoir ....Boucher
André Penvern...Policeman
Lawrence Davidson...Policeman
Maggie Scott ....Gabrielle
Hugh Quarshie...Zangaron Officer
Olu Jacobs...Customs Officer
Gyearbuor Asante ....Geoffrey (as Christopher Asante)
Thomas Baptiste ....Dexter
Eddie Tagoe ....Jinja
Kenny Ireland ....Film Crew
Jim Broadbent ....Film Crew
André Toffel ....Priest
Diana Bracho..Nun
Ilario Bisi-Pedro ....Kimba
Robert Berger ....Poker Player
William Cain ....Poker Player (as William B. Cain)
Russell Carr ....Poker Player
José Rabelo...Hotel Clerk
Victoria Tennant..Dinner Party Guest
Erica Creer ....Dinner Party Guest
Sheila Ruskin ....Dinner Party Guest
Alan Beckwith ....Mercenary

Produced by
Larry DeWaay
Norman Jewison
Patrick J. Palmer

Original music by
Geoffrey Burgon

Cinematography by
Jack Cardiff

Film Editing by
Antony Gibbs

Production Design by
Peter Mullins

Art Direction
Michael Collins
Bert Davey
John Siddall

Costume Design by
Emma Porteus (as Emma Porteous)

Makeup Department
Ramon Gow..hair stylist
Richard Mills...makeup artist
Neville Smallwood...makeup artist

Production Management
Lois Hartwick............................unit production manager: New York
Ted Lloyd...production supervisor

Second Unit Directors or Assistant Directors
Gerry Gavigan...second assistant director
Lewis Gould ....second assistant director: New York
Terry Madden...second assistant director
Michelle Marx ....first assistant director: Miami
John Robertson...............................second assistant director: Miami

Candace Suerstedt-Rehmet ....first assistant director: New York
Anthony Waye ....first assistant director

Art Department
Roy Carnon ....production illustrator
Tony Graysmark ....construction manager
Dave Jordan ....property master

Sound Department
Gordon K. McCallum.......................................chief dubbing mixer
Ivan Sharrock ....sound mixer
Ken Weston..boom operator

Special Effects
Lawrence J. Cavanaugh ....special effects (as Larry Cavanaugh)
Mike Collins ....special effects
Rudy Liszczak ....special effects
Joe Lombardi ....special effects coordinator
Steve Lombardi ....special effects

Stunts
John Ashby...stunts
Alex Brown..stunts
Lincoln McSweeney ....stunts
Roy Scammel...stunts
Eddie Smith..stunts
Eddie Stacey ....stunt co-ordinator: Europe
Marvin Walters ....stunt co-ordinator: Africa
Ray Woodford..stunts

Other crew
Barbara Allen...production coordinator
Yvonne Axeworthy ....script supervisor
Alan Beckwith.................stand-in: Christopher Walken (uncredited)
Peter Bennett ....location manager (as Peter D. Bennett)

Jack Cardiff...additional photographer
Irving Deutch.............................director of photography: New York
John Downes ....location manager
John Elton.......................................director of photography: Miami
Jane Feinberg...casting: USA
Mike Fenton..casting: USA
Susie Figgis...casting: Europe
Frank Heeney...gaffer
Peter Honess..assistant editor
David James..still photographer
Colin Manning ....camera grip
Terry Needham ....location manager
Peter Norman ......camera operator: New York (as Peter D. Norman)
Julia Pascal...location casting
Bill Pochetty ....best boy
Mike Russell ....unit publicist
Danny Shelmerdine.....................................second assistant camera
Robin Vidgeon..first assistant camera
Chic Waterson ....camera operator

Tagline: Cry 'Havoc!' And Let Slip The Dogs Of War

Run time: UK:118
Country: UK/USA
Language: English
Colour: Colour (Technicolor)
Sound Mix: Dolby
Certification: Finland:K-16/France:-12/UK:15/USA:R

Storyline: While on a reconnaissance job to the African nation of Zangora, mercenary Paul Shannon is tortured and deported. He later returns to lead a revolution in order to execute a coup designed to bring to power another, more friendly, dictator. Noted outstanding performance from: Christopher Walken.

The Fourth Protocol (1987)
Directed by John Mackenzie
Screenplay by
George Axelrod
Richard Burridge (additional material)
Frederick Forsyth
Based upon the novel by Frederick Forsyth

Cast:

Michael Caine	John Preston
Pierce Brosnan	Valeri Petrofsky
Ned Beatty	Borisov
Joanna Cassidy	Vassilievna
Julian Glover	Brian Harcourt-Smith
Michael Gough	Sir Bernard Hemmings
Ray McAnally	General Karpov
Ian Richardson	Sir Nigel Irvine
Anton Rodgers	George Berenson
Caroline Blakiston	Angela Berenson
Joseph Brady	Carmichael
Betsy Brantley	Eileen McWhirter
Sean Chapman	Captain Lyndhurst
Matt Frewer	Tom McWhirter
Jerry Harte	Professor Krilov
Michael J. Jackson	Major Pavlov
Matthew Marsh	Barry Banks
Alan North	Govershin
Ronald Pickup	Wynne-Evans
Aaron Swartz	Gregoriev
Octavia Verdin	Jill Dunkley
Johnny Allan	Night Porter
Ray Alon	Russian Seaman
Michael Bilton	Kim Philby
Sarah Bullen	Dorothy
Rebecca Burrill	Nurse

Peter Cartwright...Jan Marais
Rosy Clayton ....Mrs. Adrian
David Conville..Bursham
Nancy Crane...Karpov's Secretary
Joanna Dickens...Woman Shopper
Sam Douglas ....Russian Soldier
Mick Ford...Sergeant Bilbow
Ronnie Golden...The Busker
Steve Halliwell...Plastercast Courier
Gordon Honeycombe ....Television Announcer
John Horsley ....Sir Anthony Plumb
Boris Isarov..Dresser
Philip Jackson ....Burkinshaw
Julian Jacobson..Conductor
Alexei Jawdokimov ....Aeroflot Pilot
Clare Kelly ....Landlady
Sally Kinghorn ....Girlfriend
Ronnie Laughlin...Driver at Scene
Renos Liondaris ....Greek Cafe Owner
Peter Manning ....Violinist
Kenneth Midwood ....Chaplain
John Murtagh..Scottish Policeman
James Older ....Timmy Preston
William Parker...Cruiser
Stephen Persaud...Black Kid
George Phillips ....Mr. Adrian
Neville Phillips ....Man in Overcoat
Richard Ridings...Skinhead
Mark Rolston ....Russian Decoder
Michael Seezen ....Joey
Patsy Smart...Preston's Housekeeper
Phil Smeeton ....Boyfriend
Jirí Stanislav ....Winkler
Christopher Walker...Skinhead
Juanita Waterman ....Black Girl on Underground Train

Tariq Yunus..Immigration Officer
George Zenios...Greek Cafe Owner

Produced by
Timothy Burrill
Michael Caine (executive)
Frederick Forsyth (executive)
Wafic Said (executive)

Original music by
Lalo Schifrin
Francis Shaw

Cinematography by Phil Meheux
Film Editing by
Graham Walker

Casting
Priscilla John
Lynn Stalmaster

Production Design by
Allan Cameron
Art Direction
Tim Hutchinson

Set Decoration
Peter Howitt

Costume Design by
Tiny Nicholls

Makeup Department
Lois Burwell ....makeup department head
Peter Robb-King...makeup artist

Sound Department
Chris Munro ....sound mixer

Special Effects
Peter Hutchinson ....special effects

Stunts
Eddie Stacey ....stunt co-ordinator

Other crew
Diana Dill ....script supervisor
Steve Mcleod ....best boy
Terry Potter..gaffer
Gail Samuelson ....production coordinator

Run time: UK:119
Country: UK
Language: English
Colour: Colour
Sound Mix: Dolby

Certification: Finland:K-16/Germany:16/UK:15/USA:R

Storyline: John Preston blows the safe of a Government colleague believing – correctly – that he has been leaking secrets to the Russians. It transpires that the colleague was the victim of false flag recruitment and a plan has been conceived to plant a nuclear device near a USA airbase in Britain by Communist extremists.

John Preston has to track the device down before it's too late. Noted outstanding performances from: Michael Caine, Michael Goth and Ian Richardson.

Cry of the Innocent (1978) (TV)
Directed by Michael O'Herlihy
Screenplay by Sidney Michaels
Based upon the novel by Frederick Forsyth

Cast:

Rod Taylor	Steve Donigan
Joanna Pettet	Cynthia Donigan/Candia Leighton
Nigel Davenport	Gray Harrison Hunt
Cyril Cusack	Tom Moloney
Walter Gotell	Jack Brewster
Jim Norton	Jasper Tooms
Alexander Knox	Thornton Donegan
Tom Jordan	Buck Haggerty
Fidelma Murphy	Lady Clerk
Michael O'Sullivan	Officer Gordon
Ronnie Walsh	Pete Medwin

Run time: Germany: 93/USA: 98
Country: Ireland
Language: English
Colour: Colour

2X Frederick Forsyth (aka No Comebacks)

USA only made for TV movies based upon two short stories in Forsyth's anthology *No Comebacks*.

The productions were produced by Tara Production an Irish/US production and the stories were 'A Careful Man' and 'Privilege'.

No UK air-date was given.

The Deceiver aka Frederick Forsyth Presents (1989–90)

Note: The next set of six TV movies come under the joint title *The Deceiver*, four of which Frederick Forsyth re-wrote for his book of the same name.

Just Another Secret (1989) (TV)

Directed by Lawrence Gordon Clark
Screenplay by Murray Smith
Based upon a story by
Frederick Forsyth

Cast:

Beau Bridges	Kenneth Cranham,
James Faulkner	Erich Hallhuber
Enn Reitel	Richard Kane
Michael Ensign	Beatie Edney
Alan Howard	Thomas Wheatley
David Howey	Timothy Kightley
Carolyn Choa	Bernd Stephan
Donald Arthur	Michael Gahr
Darko Janes	Dani Segina (as Djani Segina)
Venco Kapural	Dusko Valentic
Zdenko Jelcic	Julije Perlaki
Ljubo Zecevic	Nada Abrus

Produced by
Nick Elliott (executive)
Frederick Forsyth (executive)
Frederick Muller
Murray Smith (executive)

Original music by
Paul Chihara

Cinematography by
Cristiano Pogany
Film Editing by
Alan Pattillo

Casting
Michelle Guish

Production Design by
Peter Mullins

Art Direction
Francesco Chianese

Costume Design by
Barbara Lane

Makeup Department
Giancarlo Del Brocco ....makeup supervisor
Rita Innocenzi ....hair stylist

Production Management
Donko Buljan ....production supervisor: Yugoslavia
Malcolm J. Christopher...................production supervisor (as Malcolm
Christopher)

Second Unit Directors or Assistant Directors
Chris Carreras..first assistant director
Marcia Gay..second assistant director
Justin Muller...third assistant director

Art Department
Dusko Jericevic...art director: Yugoslavia
Dave Jordan ....property master

Sound Department
Jonathan Bates..sound editor
Paul Botham ....boom operator
Gerry Humphreys ....dubbing mixer
Dick Lewzey...music recordist
Sandy MacRae...sound
Teddy Mason..dialogue editor

Special Effects
David Beavis special effects supervisor

Stunts
Marc Boyle stunt co-ordinator

Other crew
Roberto Allegretti ....gaffer

Sallie Beechinor ....production coordinator
Bill Blunden ....supervising editor
Zrinka Buljan............................production coordinator: Yugoslavia
Jamie Christopher..production runner
Joseph D'Agosta..casting: USA
Velinka Ficor ....production coordinator: Yugoslavia
Ray Freeborn ....location manager
Brian Gascoigne...music associate
Jack King...production accountant
Christopher Lloyd................................assistant film editor
Valerie Nelson ....production associate
Silvia Pyke ....contact: London
June Randall ....script supervisor
Bob Robinson..assistant film editor
Gianni Savini ....key grip
Luciano Tonti ....camera operator
Don Worts..production buyer
Michael Yell...location accountant

Run time: USA:100
Country: UK
Language: English
Colour: Colour (Technicolor)
Certification: USA:PG

Pride and Extreme Prejudice (1989) (TV)
Directed by Ian Sharp
Screenplay by Murray Smith
Based upon a story by Frederick Forsyth

Cast:
Brian Dennehy ....Simon Cadell
Lisa Eichhorn ....Leonie Mellinger
Michael Shannon...Malcolm Storry
Sabina Trooger ....Alan Howard
Sebastian Baur..Patrick Pearson

Tony Doyle..Eamon Boland
Guy Deghy..Anne Dyson
Niven Boyd ....Jill Spurrier
Brian Hickey ....Peggy Lukac
Dorothea Moritz...Tom Deininger
Anton Rattinger ....Christian Giese
Jockel Tschiersch...Peter Kortenbach

Produced by
Nick Elliott (executive)
Frederick Forsyth (executive)
Frederick Muller
Murray Smith (executive)

Original music by
Paul Chihara

Cinematography by
Cristiano Pogany
Film Editing by
Alan Pattillo

Casting
Michelle Guish

Production Design by
Peter Mullins

Art Direction
Fred Carter

Costume Design by
Barbara Lane

Makeup Department
Giancarlo Del Brocco ....makeup supervisor

Rita Innocenzi ....hair stylist

Production Management
Malcolm J. Christopher ....production supervisor (as Malcolm Christopher)
Michael Schwarz production supervisor: Germany

Second Unit Directors or Assistant Directors
Chris Carreras..first assistant director
Marcia Gay...second assistant director
Justin Muller..third assistant director

Art Department
Albrecht Konrad.....................┬.........................art director: Germany
John Park ....construction manager
Arthur Wicks...property master

Sound Department
Jonathan Bates...sound editor
Paul Botham ....boom operator
Gerry Humphreys .... dubbing mixer
Dick Lewzey...music recordist
Sandy MacRae...sound
Teddy Mason...dialogue editor

Special Effects
David Beavis special effects supervisor

Stunts
Marc Boyle   stunt co-ordinator

Other crew
Roberto Allegretti ....gaffer
Ken Ashley-Johnson ....key grip
Sallie Beechinor ....production coordinator
Bill Blunden ....supervising editor

Peter Carter..location manager
Jamie Christopher...production runner
Joseph D'Agosta...casting: USA
Alan Flyng..wardrobe master
Ray Freeborn ....location manager
Brian Gascoigne..music associate
Jack King..production accountant
Christopher Lloyd...assistant film editor
Valerie Nelson ....production associate
Bill Pochetty...best boy (as Billy Pochetty)
Silvia Pyke ....contact: London
June Randall ....script supervisor
Bob Robinson ....assistant film editor
Gabi Scheiger ....production coordinator: Germany
Luciano Tonti ....camera operator
Don Worts..production buyer
Michael Yell..location accountant

Run time: USA:92
Country: UK
Language: English
Colour: Colour (Technicolor)
Certification: USA:PG

Little Piece of Sunshine (1990) (TV)
Directed by James Cellan Jones
Screenplay by Murray Smith
Based upon a story by Frederick Forsyth

Cast:
Larry Lam ....Chris Cooper
Philip Michael Thomas...Kitty Aldridge
Lauren Bacall ....Alan Howard
Clarence Thomas ....Robert MacBeth
W. Paul Bodie..Nelson Oramas
Luis Alday...Ed Amatrudo

Jay Amor...John Archie
Philip Astor ....Alston L. Bair
June Barr...Julian Bevans
Rex King ....Chris McCarty
Abraham Meeks..Ronald Shelley

Produced by
Nick Elliott (executive)
Frederick Forsyth (executive)
Frederick Muller
Murray Smith (executive)

Original music by
Paul Chihara

Cinematography by
Cristiano Pogany

Film Editing by
Alan Pattillo

Production Design by
Peter Mullins

Art Direction
Frederic C. Weiler (as Frederick Weiler)

Costume Design by
Lynette Bernay

Makeup Department
Jay Cannistraci.....................................makeup artist: Lauren Bacall
Marie Del Russo ....makeup supervisor
Diane Johnson ....hair stylist

Production Management
Malcolm J. Christopher....................................production supervisor
(as Malcolm Christopher)
Linda McGowan ....unit production manager

Second Unit Directors or Assistant Directors
Alan Berger ....third assistant director
Douglas Bruce..................second assistant director (as Doug Bruce)
Gino Marotta ....first assistant director

Art Department
Charles Guanci Jr.................property master (as Charlie Guanci Jr.)
Carl Ritz...construction manager

Sound Department
Jonathan Bates..sound editor
Jack Dalton ....boom operator
Gerry Humphreys ....dubbing mixer
Teddy Mason...dialogue editor
Mike Tromer...sound recordist

Stunts
Mark Mercury ....stunt co-ordinator (as Marc Mercury)
Robert Paisley ....stunts
Other crew
Fabio Arber...location manager
Bill Blunden ....supervising editor
Jack Cowden..script supervisor
Joseph D'Agosta...casting: Los Angeles
Michael Dock...casting: Miami
Guz Holzer ....coordinator: Bimini
Craig Hundley...music associate
Ellen Jacoby...casting: Miami
Marilyn Johnson ....casting: UK
Cary Jones...key grip

Jack King..production accountant
Mark Lafata..production coordinator
Christopher Lloyd...assistant film editor
William Loger ....wardrobe supervisor
Malcolm MacIntosh ....camera operator
Valerie Nelson ....production associate
Silvia Pyke ....contact: London
Bob Robinson...assistant film editor
Gary Ryan ....gaffer
Michael Yell...location accountant

Run time: USA:96

The Price of the Bride (1990) (TV)
Directed by Tom Clegg
Screenplay by Murray Smith

Cast:
Mike Farrel ....Peter Egan
Robert Foxworth...Diana Quick
Alan Howard...David Healy
Bruno Dietrich...Don Fellows
Ron Berglas ....Colin Bruce
Michael Eaves...Clyde Gatell
Gay Baynes...Heather James
Sarah Rhoades...Timothy Block

Produced by
Nick Elliott (executive)
Frederick Forsyth (executive)
Frederick Muller
Murray Smith (executive)

Original music by
Paul Chihara

Cinematography by
Cristiano Pogany

Film Editing by
Alan Pattillo

Casting
Marilyn Johnson

Production Design by
Peter Mullins

Art Direction
Robin Tarsnane

Costume Design by
Barbara Lane

Makeup Department
Giancarlo Del Brocco..makeup artist
Rita Innocenzi ....hair stylist

Production Management
Malcolm J. Christopher .... production supervisor (as Malcolm
Christopher)
Second Unit Director or Assistant Director
Gino Marotta ....first assistant director
Justin Muller..third assistant director

Art Department
Malcolm Roberts ....construction manager
Graham Stickley ....property master

Sound Department
Jonathan Bates...sound editor
Paul Botham ....boom operator

Gerry Humphreys ....dubbing mixer
Sandy MacRae...sound
Teddy Mason..dialogue editor

Special Effects
David Beavis...special effects supervisor

Stunts
Marc Boyle ....stunt co-ordinator

Other crew
Roberto Allegretti ....gaffer
Ken Ashley-Johnson ....key grip
Sallie Beechinor ....production coordinator
Bill Blunden ....supervising editor
Peter Carter...location manager
Joseph D'Agosta..casting: USA
Warren Ewen..best boy gaffer
Alan Flyng..wardrobe master
Ray Freeborn ....location manager
Craig Hundley ....music associate
Jack King...production accountant
Christopher Lloyd..assistant film editor
Valerie Nelson ....production associate
Silvia Pyke ....contact: London
June Randall ....script supervisor
Bob Robinson ....assistant film editor
Luciano Tonti ....camera operator
Don Worts...production buyer
Michael Yell...location accountant

Run time: USA:97
Country: UK
Language: English
Colour: Colour (Technicolor)
Certification: USA:PG

Country: UK
Language: English
Colour: Colour (Technicolor)
Certification: USA:PG

A Casualty of War (1990) (TV)
Directed by Tom Clegg
Screenplay by Murray Smith
Based upon the story by Frederick Forsyth

Cast

David Threlfall	Shelley Hack
Amanda Burton	Richard Hope
Clarke Peters	Nadim Sawalha
Alan Howard	James Donnelly
Vincent Murphy	John Keegan
Bill Bailey	Hubert Kramer
Geoffrey Whitehead	Allan Mitchell
Simon Gregor	Walter McMonagle
Tessa Wojtczak	Janez Vajevec

Produced by
Nick Elliott (executive)
Frederick Forsyth (executive)
Frederick Muller
Murray Smith

Original music by
Paul Chihara

Cinematography by
Cristiano Pogany

Film Editing by
Alan Pattillo

Casting
Michelle Guish

Production Design by
Peter Mullins
Art Direction
Fred Carter
Francesco Chianese

Costume Design by
Barbara Lane

Makeup Department
Giancarlo Del Brocco ....makeup supervisor
Rita Innocenzi ....hair stylist

Production Management
Donko Buljan ....production supervisor: Yugoslavia
Malcolm J. Christopher...................................production supervisor

Second Unit Directors or Assistant Directors
Gianni Cozzo..first assistant director
Justin Muller..third assistant director
Art Department
Dusko Jericevic...art director: Yugoslavia
John Park ....construction manager
Arthur Wicks...property master

Sound Department
Jonathan Bates...sound editor
Paul Botham ....boom operator
Gerry Humphreys ....dubbing mixer
Dick Lewzey..music recordist
Sandy MacRae..sound recordist
Teddy Mason..dialogue editor

Special Effects
David Beavis..special effects supervisor

Stunts
Marc Boyle ....stunt co-ordinator

Other crew
Roberto Allegretti ....gaffer
Ken Ashley-Johnson ....key grip
Sallie Beechinor ....production coordinator
Bill Blunden ....supervising editor
Zrinka Buljan.............................production coordinator: Yugoslavia
Peter Carter...location manager
Jamie Christopher...production runner
Joseph D'Agosta...casting: USA
Velinka Ficor ....production coordinator: Yugoslavia
Alan Flyng..wardrobe master
Ray Freeborn ....location manager
Brian Gascoigne...music associate
Jack King...production accountant
Christopher Lloyd...assistant film editor
Valerie Nelson ....production associate
Bill Pochetty..best boy (as Billy Pochetty)
Silvia Pyke ....contact: London
June Randall ....script supervisor
Bob Robinson...assistant film editor
Gianni Savini ....key grip
Luciano Tonti ....camera operator
Don Worts..production buyer
Michael Yell..location accountant

Run time: USA:96
Country: UK
Language: English
Colour: Colour (Technicolor)
Certification: USA:PG

Death Has a Bad Reputation (1990) (TV)
Directed by Lawrence Gordon Clark
Screenplay by Murray Smith
Based upon a story by Frederick Forsyth

Cast:
Tony Lo Bianco ....Pamela Villoresi
Elizabeth Hurley ....Gottfried John
Alan Howard..Venantino Venantini
David Lyon ....Sabina Trooger
Udo Vioff..Guy Scantlebury
Richard Hope ....Garrick Hagon
Philip Lowrie..Pier Luigi Misasi
Marzia Ubaldi ....Roberto Sbaratto
Roberto Renna ....Ilza Prestinari
Mark Gellard...Massimo Sarchielli

Produced by
Nick Elliott (executive)
Frederick Forsyth (executive)
Frederick Muller
Murray Smith (executive)
Original music by
Paul Chihara

Cinematography by
Cristiano Pogany

Film Editing by
Alan Pattillo

Casting
Michelle Guish

Production Design by
Peter Mullins

Art Direction
Fred Carter
Francesco Chianese

Costume Design by
Barbara Lane

Makeup Department
Giancarlo Del Brocco ....makeup supervisor
Rita Innocenzi ....hair stylist

Production Management
Malcolm J. Christopher....................................production supervisor
Paolo Lucidi...production supervisor: Italy

Second Unit Directors or Assistant Directors
Justin Muller...third assistant director
Luciano Sacripanti...first assistant director

Art Department
Arthur Wicks...property master
Sound Department
Jonathan Bates...sound editor
Paul Botham ....boom operator
Gerry Humphreys ....dubbing mixer
Sandy MacRae...sound recordist
Teddy Mason...dialogue editor

Special Effects
David Beavis...special effects supervisor

Stunts
Marc Boyle ....stunt co-ordinator
Stefano Maria Mioni ....stunts (uncredited)

Other crew
Roberto Allegretti ....gaffer

Sallie Beechinor ....production coordinator
Bill Blunden ....editorial supervisor
Alfredo Bocci ....wardrobe master
Francesco Cinieri...casting: Italy
Enrico Coletti ....location manager
Joseph D'Agosta...casting: USA
Ray Freeborn ....location manager
Craig Hundley ....music associate
Jack King..production accountant
Christopher Lloyd...assistant film editor
Giovanni Lovatelli..location manager
Janice Munro...production coordinator: Italy
Valerie Nelson ....production associate
Silvia Pyke ....contact: London
June Randall ....script supervisor
Bob Robinson...assistant film editor
Gianni Savini ....key grip
Enzo Sisti ....production accountant: Italy
Luciano Tonti ....camera operator
Michael Yell...location accountant

Run time: USA:98
Country: UK
Language: English
Colour: Colour (Technicolor)
Certification: USA:PG

The Day of the Devil (1995)
Indian movie loosely based upon Frederick Forsyth's novel
The Day of the Jackal

Code Name: Wolverine (1996) (TV)
Directed by David Jackson
Screenplay by Robert T. Megginson
Based upon a story by Frederick Forsyth

Cast:
Urbano Barberini
Eric Bassanesi
Alessandro Borgese
Richard Brooks ....Cyrus Cassell
Tom Collins..Matthew Cox
Robert M Dawson...Deborah De Furia
Alessio Di Clemente...Sam Douglas
David Israel ....Traci Lind
Noah Margetts...Andrew Lord Miller
Brobbie Milowsky...Stefano Maria Mioni
Brian Protheroe..Danny Quinn
Ted Roussoff ....Antonio Sabato Jr
Richard Sharp ....Francesco Siciliano
Ramon Tikaram...Jeffry Wickham

Country: USA

Language: English

Colour: Colour

DOCUMENTARIES

Soldiers – The History of Men in Battle (1985)

Narrated by Frederick Forsyth

BBC and Channel 7

Written by John Keegan and Richard Holmes

Series screened from 25 September 1985

Frederick Forsyth
Bibliography

WHAT FOLLOWS is a guide to collecting the published work of Frederick Forsyth. You will find detailed the earliest and most unusual variations of his books.

The guide essentially details UK issues. This is because Forsyth's novels are first published there and, essentially, the most collectable variants. There are, of course, exceptions to this rule, and a selection of these titles are also listed.

This guide is by no means exhaustive. It is, however, one of the most comprehensive published and clearly shows the many different collectable formats Forsyth's books have taken.

COLLECTING FREDERICK FORSYTH
Key
(a note to some of the abbreviations used in this guide)
ISBN = International Standard Book Number
h/b = hard back
d/w= dust wrapper
p/b = paper back
c/w= crepe wrap

First Editions
(all first editions listed are h/b d/w unless marked*)
*The Biafra Story**. Penguin Special p/b, 1969.
The Day of the Jackal. Hutchinson, 1971.
The Odessa File. Hutchinson, 1972.

The Dogs of War. Hutchinson, 1974.

The Shepherd (illustrated novella). Hutchinson, 1975.

The Devil's Alternative. Hutchinson, 1979.

No Comebacks: anthology of short stories, including: No Comebacks, There Are No Snakes in Ireland, The Emperor, There Are Some Days..., Money With Menaces, Used in Evidence, Privilege, Duty, A Careful Man, Sharp Practice): Hutchinson, 1982.

The Fourth Protocol. Hutchinson, 1984.

The Negotiator. Bantam Press, 1989.

The Deceiver. Bantam Press, 1991.

The Fist of God. Bantam Press, 1994.

Icon. Bantam Press, 1996.

The Phantom of Manhattan. Bantam Press, 1999.

Quintet. (Internet book published in five monthly parts by Online Originals 2000 and 2001, A4 paper download with pictorial title page for each story.)

The Veteran. Bantam Press, 2001.

Anthologies

The Novels of Frederick Forsyth (*The Day of the Jackal, The Odessa File, The Dogs of War*) (includes a special introduction by the author). Hutchinson, 1978.

Frederick Forsyth: Forsyth's First Three (*The Day of the Jackal, The Odessa File, The Dogs of War*). Viking Press, 1980.

Frederick Forsyth: Three Complete Detective Novels (*The Day of the Jackal, The Odessa File, The Dogs of War*). Avenel, 1980.

Frederick Forsyth – The Four Novels (*The Day of the Jackal, The Odessa File, The Dogs of War, The Devil's Alternative*) (includes a special introduction by the author). Hutchinson, 1982.

The Frederick Forsyth Collection (*The Fourth Protocol, The Devil's Alternative, No Comebacks*). St Michaels, 1984.

The Frederick Forsyth Anthology (includes abridged versions of *The Day of the Jackal, The Odessa File, The Dogs of War, The Devil's Alternative*). Reader's Digest, 1996.

Signed Limited Editions

The Dogs of War (USA 1st edition, signed in a limited edition for the First Edition Circle). Viking, h/b d/w, 1974.

No Comebacks and Other Stories. (Shorter version of anthology including: No Comebacks, There Are Some Days..., Money With Menaces. Numbered in an edition of 350 copies signed by the author.) Eurographic, p/b d/w, 1982.

The Fourth Protocol (numbered in an edition of 600 copies signed by the author, h/b in slip case). Brandywyne, 1984.

The Day of the Jackal (signed leatherette bound h/b edition, illustrated by Christopher Zacharow. Unsigned version also available.) Franklin Mystery Library, 1987.

The Negotiator (numbered in an edition of 150 copies signed by the author). London Limited Editions, h/b c/w, 1989.

The Phantom of Manhattan (signed Morocco leather bound h/b with Ribbon bookmark. Foreward by Andrew Lloyd Webber and illustrated by Bruce Waldman. Unsigned version also available). Franklin Library, 1990.

Proofs

(paperbacks with wraps.)

The Day of the Jackal. Hutchinson, 1971.

The Odessa File. Hutchinson, 1972.

The Dogs of War. Hutchinson, 1974.

The Devil's Alternative. Hutchinson, 1979.

No Comebacks. Hutchinson, 1982.

The Fourth Protocol. Hutchinson, 1984.

The Negotiator. Bantam Press, 1989.

The Deceiver. Bantam Press, 1991.

The Fist of God. Bantam Press, 1994.

Icon. Bantam Press, 1996.

(*Note:* various overseas trade paperbacks and advance reading copies/proofs also exist.)

Early Editions
(easily detected by different ISBNs.)
The Negotiator: ISBN0552135550.
The Fist of God: ISBN0552142344.
The Veteran: ISBN0593048954

Open Market Editions
(easily detected by different ISBNs.)
The Fourth Protocol: ISBN055212687X.
The Negotiator: ISBN0552135542.

Large Print Editions
The Day of the Jackal. Chivers Press.
The Deceiver. Ulverscroft.
Great Flying Stories. Mary Wheller.
The Phantom of Manhattan. Chivers Press.
(Most large print companies – as well as Forsyth's main publishers – stock audio books of major novels, some – especially large print publishers – include unabridged text.)

Library Editions
The Biafra Story – The Making of an African Legend. (Full-length text with specially commissioned Foreword and Afterword by the author. Of extra note as it was the first hardback copy of *The Biafra Story*, the previous two editions being paperbacks.) Severn House, 1983.

Library Sheets
(unbound copies of individual books supplied to libraries for in-house binding)
   The Negotiator (ISBN0593016491)
   The Deceiver (ISBN059302348X)
   The Fist of God (ISBN0593040864)
   The Phantom of Manhattan (ISBN0593045653)

Contributions

Great Flying Stories (Introduction only). Bellew, 1991.

Soldiers – An Illustrated History of Men in Battle. Foreword by Frederick Forsyth. John Keegan and Richard Holmes. h/b d/w, 1985.

Reflections on Fishing in Childhood (various contributions). Summersdale Publishers, h/b d/w, 1995.

Crime Movies (various contributions). Severn House, h/b d/w, 1996.

Airlift to Biafra. Tony Byrne. The Columba Press, p/b, 1997.

Hugo Manning: Poet and Humanist. Ivan Savidge, etc. Open Gate Press, h/b d/w, 1997.

Britain Held Hostage. (Special Foreword by Frederick Forsyth.) *Lindsay Jenkins.* Orange State Press, p/b, 1998.

Freedom (various contributions) (charity book in association with the British Red Cross) 2000. (Anthology of works connected to the Biafra War.)

Dictionary of Dangerous Words. Digby Anderson. Politico's, 2000.

Miscellaneous Collector's Editions

The Making of an African Legend: The Biafra Story (updated version, different cover to original issue). Penguin Books p/b, 1977.

Great Flying Stories (Corgi p/b, 1994) (includes *The Shepherd*).

Note: Not all copies of *Great Flying Stories* included Forsyth's novella *The Shepherd*, which consequently means that his comments appertaining to it are cut from his Introduction.

Icon: book club size format, but originates from main publisher) (ISBN0593041593). Bantam Press, 1996.

Britain and Europe: speech delivered at the Tenth Ian Gow Memorial Lecture by Frederick Forsyth, CBE) (2000).

Note: other lectures by Frederick Forsyth can be downloaded from the web; however '*Britain and Europe*' is the only official lecture bound for retail sale

The Biafra Story: The Making of an African Legend. Pen & Sword, 2002.*

*This book is currently being negotiated as I compile this bibliography, and its title and publication date could possibly change. This entry serves only for information purposes.

Reader's Digest Condensed Versions
(Although abridged from Forsyth's original text, these books are still collectable, as most include colour illustrations).
The Day of the Jackal 1972.
The Odessa File 1973.
The Dogs of War 1974.
The Devil's Alternative 1979.
The Fourth Protocol 1984.
The Negotiator 1990.
The Deceiver 1992.
The Fist of God 1994.
Icon 1997.

Important note: Reader's Digest would like to state that they do not hold copies of the above titles in stock. Collectors wishing to obtain copies are advised to advertise or seek the talents of a good book searcher.

It is also unlikely that other publishing houses mentioned in this guide hold original stock, as all copies are generally sold out on first publication.

Appendices

Appendix I
Original interview material

This book was based upon eight exclusive interviews with Frederick Forsyth, as follows:

November 1999, March 2000, July 2000, August 2000, September 2000, February 2001, March 2001, April 2001.

Other interviews included:
Lord Janner of Brunstone, January 2001; Lord Andrew Lloyd Webber, March 2001; Michael Heseltine, October 2000; Ed Victor, April 2001; George Jesse Turner, May 2000; Edward Fox, November 2000; Sir Derek Jacobi, February 2001; John 'Cats Eyes' Cunningham, November 1999; Craig Thomas, 1994; Campbell Armstrong, 1992, Ian Rankin, March 2001.

Appendix II
Copyright Credits